ON DEMONOLOGY AND WITCHCRAFT IN CEYLON

ON DEMONOLOGY AND WITCHCRAFT IN CEYLON

DANDRIS DE SILVA GOONERATNE

GYAN

Published by

GYAN

Gyan Publishing House
5, Ansari Road
Daryaganj, New Delhi-110002
Phone: 011-47034999, 9811692060
E-mail: books@gyanbooks.com

Distribution Network
gyanbooks.com
India, USA, Canada, UK, Australia, France

ISBN : 978-81-212-3843-4 (PB)
First Published, Colombo, 1865

2nd Impression 2020

Printed at: Gyan Press, Delhi.

On Demonology and Witchcraft in Ceylon
Author: Dandris De Silva Gooneratne

On Demonology and Witchcraft in Ceylon.—By Dandris De Silva Gooneratne, Modliar.

General Remarks on Demon Worship.

A belief in the realities of an invisible world of evil spirits as influencing, in a certain manner, many of the ordinary concerns of human life, has not only always formed an integral part of the creed of a large majority of mankind in every age and country of the world, but has also had, and still has, to a considerable extent, a certain strange, mysterious, and unaccountable fascination for the mind of man, even when reason happens to raise its authoritative voice of condemnation against it. Why, or how this is so—whether it is founded on any innate, morbid quality of the human heart, which men find it difficult to resist under certain circumstances, or on any intrinsic truth inherent in the nature of the thing itself, or only on mere ignorance, it is as far from my present purpose, as it is beyond my humble abilities, to discuss here. But that the belief really exists will hardly admit of a doubt.

This belief has, according to the amount of intelligence and civilization possessed by those among whom it prevails, given rise to various systems of superstition, of which some are of the most debasing and revolting character. And although there is scarcely a single country in the world, in which this belief does not more or less prevail in some form or other, yet we do not think there is any, in which it has developed itself in such gigantic proportions, or such hideous forms, as in this beautiful Island. Elsewhere it may sometimes exercise considerable influence and even command many devoted votaries; but here it has been moulded into a regular *religion*, arranged and methodized into a system, and carefully preserved in writing: so that the amount of influence, which it exercises over the thoughts, the habits, the every day life of a Singhalese, is such as can hardly be believed by a stranger to the character of a genuine Singhalese Buddhist.

A series of writers commencing with Knox and ending with Sir Emerson Tennent, have, at different periods, during the last 200 years, given to the public the results of their enquiries and experience in matters connected with this Island, in a number of interesting and able works of which Sir Emerson's is the last and the greatest: yet none of these writers seem to have perceived, in any *adequate* degree, the extraordinary amount of gross superstition which prevails among the people, of whose manners, customs, and history they professed to treat; not that they have omitted to mention the worship of gods and demons, as well as Buddhism and a few other superstition, as existing among our countrymen, and even in some instances, gone into considerable details *respecting them*, but they do not appear to have been fully aware of the extraordinary degree of influence they exercise over the mind of a Singhalese. This is owing partly to the circumstance of these writers being Englishmen, mostly unacquainted with the native languages, and partly to a certain reluctance, which a demon-worshipper always feels, to communicate full and unreserved information to a stranger who professes a different religion, suspecting that the object of the Englishman, in seeking for information respecting a system in which he himself does not believe, is only to publish it in his books and newspapers, and thereby expose it to public ridicule.

In the following pages, we propose to class the different forms of superstition prevailing among our countrymen, under the following heads, viz:—I. DEMONISM, or the worship of demons or evil spirits; II. CAPUISM, or the worship of gods, demigods, and deified heroes; III. GRAHAISM, or the worship of planets and stars; IV. MISCELLANEOUS SUPERSTITIONS, or such as cannot properly be classed under any of the preceding heads. Not only will each of these be found to be distinct from the rest in all material points, but they also appear to have originated in the Island at different periods of time.

It is not easy, however, to fix definitely any particular period of time as that in which any of these systems of superstition *first* originated in the Island, no positive information of a very reliable character being supplied by any records of native annals now extant. Nevertheless the most reasonable supposition, and one which is supported by all who have touched upon the subject, and, to a certain extent, by the native historical records themselves, is, that the greater portion of them existed here at a very early period, long anterior to the commencement of the Christian era.

With the exception of Buddhism (also which is partly, though in some few respects only, based upon Brahminism) every species of superstition, science, or literature, which exists among the Singhalese, with certain exceptions of minor importance, may be traced, more or less directly to Brahminism and its Vedas and Shasters. Whether this is solely a consequence of Wijeyo's invasion (543 B. C.), or whether any portion of them, such as the worship of demons and of planets, had existed here even before that event, and only became assimilated to the Brahminical doctrines itself in subsequent times, it is not easy to decide; but yet, if the wild, ignorant savages, who inhabited this Island, when Wijeyo landed on it, and whom Native Chroniclers have styled *demons*, did profess any form of worship, as no doubt they must have done, it is more likely that it related to demons and planets, than to any thing else. Men steeped in complete barbarism and ignorance, separated by their insular position from the rest of the world, attributing, with the first impulse of uneducated nature, a supernatural agency to natural causes and events, when these were beyond the comprehension of their simple intellects, and naturally impelled, therefore, in the absence of any other form of religion calculated to fill up the void in their minds; to embrace any which their untutored passions and feelings, and their immediate wants and conveniences suggested to them, as the best—men such as these are likely to coin for themselves a religion, which in every respect corresponds with their own dispositions. Sickness and death, the most direful calamities of life, with the many dreadful circumstances generally attending them, are, of all causes, those which would naturally, in those early ages of the world, excite, in an ignorant and simple mind, feelings of supernatural terror; and the rise, among such a people, of a system of worship, in which every form of disease and suffering is attributed to the agency of demons, must cease to excite wonder in any mind. If Demonism did actually exist here previous to the invasion of Wijeyo, as we think it did, a multitude of other causes and circumstances, which followed that event, as consequences of it, must have cooperated to bring it into its present condition, with its charms and spells and invocations to the Hindoo deities. These changes appear to have been going on till within the last 3 centuries.

But though we are not able to fix the exact period at which Demonism originated in the Island, we have enough of evidence to prove, that its origin could not have been later than the fifth century; for the seventh Chapter of *Maha Wanse*, a work whose authenticity has never been called in question, makes mention of *Balli** offerings, made to demons at the time of Wijeyo, that is five and a half centuries before the Christian Era; which shews, that, even if Demon-worship did not prevail here in the days of Wijeyo, it did so

* Although the books of the demon priests direct that a *balli* or image of any demon invoked on any occasion, should be formed, and offerings be made to it, yet in point of practice this image, or *balli*, has generally been dispensed with in modern times.

There is another species of *balli* made to represent, not demons, but *Planet gods*. These will come to be noticed under the head *Grahaism*.

in the days of Maha Nama Terunnanse, who was engaged in the composition of that historical work, between the years 459 and 477 A. D., that is nearly 1400 years ago.

Grahaism may, with equal reason, be supposed to have been a system of still more ancient origin; the sun, moon, and stars being the first objects of wonder, which are calculated to rouse, in an ignorant mind, feelings of superstitious adoration. But, as it at present exists, it appears to be almost wholly an emanation from Brahminism. While Capuism, on the other hand, is a mixture of Hindooism and of a more refined species of Demonism, the first derived from the continent, the latter of indigenous growth, and both mixed together into a heterogeneous system, originating probably at a period later than the two former.

Although Buddha is said to have visited Ceylon three several times before its conquest by Wijeyo, his religion was not established in it till the reign of Dewanan Piatisse, who ascended the throne 307 B. C., nearly 236 years after Buddha's death. But, from the first day of its introduction into the Island, its success seems to have been very rapid; and indeed from the despotic nature of the government, and the religious enthusiasm of the king, assisted as it was by the proselytizing spirit of Dharma Soka of India (the grandson of him who has been called *Sandracòtta* by the Greek writers) its success could not but have been certain, immediate, and complete. But demonism was not displaced by it. It only took a subordinate rank. Buddhism acknowledges the existence of demons, and connives at, if it does not openly countenance, the practice of demon-worship, or at least of a great deal which belongs to it. Buddhism does not hold out worldly advantages or immediate rewards in this life to its votaries, so much as demonism does. Its task is the graver one, of pointing out a way (though an erroneous one) of obtaining salvation for the soul; an object which is to be attained, only after passing through many transmigrations of the soul, through countless millions of years—a consummation, therefore which, however devoutly wished for by a Buddhist, is still one to be attained only in another state of existence, at some unknown distant period of time. Demonism, on the other hand, deals with the concerns of this life, and of this life alone. This, therefore, appeals more strongly to the passions and feelings, in as much as it relates to things nearer and present. Hence, demonism never lost its hold on men's minds, but, on the contrary, it still continues to be the most popular of all forms of worship prevailing among the Singhalese.

The period, at which demonism seems to have been fashioned into the form it still retains, is that which intervened between the eleventh and the sixteenth centuries, during which, owing to the numerous wars which were incessantly waged between the princes of this Island and those of Southern India, thousands of Malabars often became residents, as captive slaves or as freemen, among the Singhalese, and imparted to the latter, many of their own peculiar superstitions and notions, so that many fresh additions were made to demonism, both in the number of demons, and, especially, in the introduction of a large number of charms or spells recited at every demon ceremony now; so much, indeed, does this appear to have been the case that more than seven-eighths of the charms, belonging to Singhalese Necromancy, are in the Tamil language; a circumstance which has led many to believe, that demonism is altogether an importation from the continent. During the last three centuries, no changes whatever seem to have been made in it, or if any, only of a very trifling nature, and that too, more in the gradual alterations of the language used in the invocations, than in any thing else. Knox's short account of the form of demon-worship, which prevailed at the time he was a captive in this Island, that is 200 years ago, seems, judging even from the little he has said on the subject, to be exactly the form of worship, which at this day prevails among the people.

Thus, besides Buddhism, properly so called, there are three other forms of worship, which enter into the religious creed of a Singhalese, namely Demonism, Capuism, and Grahaism. In addition to these, there are also a variety of other minor superstitions, considered to be quite necessary to his welfare, and which, though of minor importance, do engage, and will continue to engage, his serious attention, so long as he continues to be a Buddhist. As the first of these, viz., Buddhism, relates only to his spiritual interests, affecting him in another life, so the last three concern his temporal interests in this life; the fruits of the first being tasted only in another state of existence, while those of the last are enjoyed immediately and during every moment of this life. To which of these therefore a Singhalese resorts oftenest, and with the greatest eagerness, it is easy to imagine. He has one religion for his soul, and another for his body, both highly reverenced, and maintained as essential to his well being; a convenience which, as far as we are aware, no other nation in the world possesses.

The most remarkable feature in the character of a Singhalese is, not that he is a follower of any one of these superstitious systems, but that he is a follower of each and all of them at one and the same time; for the doctrines of some of these appear to be contradictory to, and inconsistent with, each other. For instance, Grahaism maintains, that the movements of the Planets influence man in every thing; that sometimes they bring disease, death, poverty and every other imaginable misery, not only on himself, but sometimes even on those connected with him; that at other times they give him health, wealth, honours, happiness, and every thing else desirable; but that all the aforesaid calamities may be prevented by propitiating the planets by certain ceremonies. On the other hand, the fundamental doctrine of the religion of Buddha, being, that every man is what he is, owing to *Karma*, that is, to the nature of what he has done, good or bad, in a previous state of existence, Buddhism, or at least every Buddhist Priest admits, in a spirit of compromise, as it were, that many of the calamities or turns of good fortune, which befall men, do take place according to the movements of the planets, but contend, that these movements are not arbitrary and optional with the planets themselves; that they are the result of a certain fixed order according to which the planets must move; that the planets are only a sort of intermediate agents, serving merely as blind instruments in the hands of *Karma*, to prefigure to the world the various changes of fortune, which must come upon each man according to his *Karma*, that is, according to his good or bad deeds in a former life; and that no propitiation of the planets, or of any power whatsoever, in the whole universe, can ward off calamities, or hinder happiness and prosperity, deserved by a man on account of this inexorable Karma. Nevertheless, a Singhalese contrives to believe in all the four systems, and to be, at the same time, recognized as an orthodox Buddhist; and it would be a rare thing to meet with any one, who, in point of practice, is a votary of only one or two of the systems. The influence which these systems command, notwithstanding such inconsistencies as the above, may be judged of from the fact, that the Buddhist Priest himself, the very teacher and expounder of the religion of Buddha, has sometimes recourse to Grahaism and even to Demonism. Before we proceed further, we shall make a few more general remarks on each of these systems.

I. DEMONISM is regarded as a means of guarding against sickness, and of curing it when it is supposed, as it almost always is, to be caused by a demon, and also as a means, in the hands of any man, of inflicting death, disease, or other calamity, on other men. A subordinate object of it is the accomplishment of purposes different from the above, such as that of protecting the fruits of a tree from pillage, of creating discord and hatred between the different members of a family, of gaining the affections of a woman, of discovering treasures hidden in the ground, and other similar purposes. The demons are regarded as beings only influenced by the worst of motives towards mankind, without a sentiment of pity, justice, or kindness, in their nature. They are made instrumental in curing diseases, as well as in inflicting them. They are to be coerced by spells, and propitiated with offerings and particular ceremonies. They cannot affect the spiritual welfare of a man in any way; but can only cause death at the most. A Singhalese demon, therefore, is a different kind of being from the demon of European superstitions or from the Diabolus of the New Testament. For, while the object of the latter is to ruin for ever the soul of a man, that of the former is only to injure the body. A Singhalese demon is himself a being subject to death, like all other beings recognised by Buddhism, although that event may in some instances take place only at the end of some tens of thousands of years. This difference arises from the Buddhist doctrine, that there is no state of perpetual existence for any being; that happiness or misery can never be perpetual; that the rewards or punishments for the actions of one life will be reaped in one or more states of existence afterwards, and then come to an end; and that mere obedience to a demon does not necessitate any disobedience to one's religion.

In every other form of worship, which exists among men, whether it be Buddhism, Capuism, Mohammedanism, Brahminism, or any other, the objects of worship are always regarded with feelings of veneration by their votaries; but in Demonism alone, no such feelings exist in the heart of the worshipper, whose worship consists only in trying to induce them by flattery, and offerings, or to coerce them by threats, to cure, or to inflict some disease, or to secure a man from becoming liable to it at all. And yet neither the rites of Buddhism, nor of Capuism, nor even of Grahaism, are more frequently and eagerly resorted to, than those belonging to the worship of demons, who, instead of being objects of religious veneration, are only objects of indescribable dread.

One of the main differences between an educated and an uneducated intellect seems to be this—that, while the former always aims at analysis, at generalization, at resolving the mysterious and the marvellous into natural causes, at laying open the hidden and inscrutable things of nature, the latter takes the directly opposite course of indulging in the unreasonable and unaccountable pleasure of throwing a veil of mystery and darkness even over those things, which, if it were to view them rationally, it might understand, and of endeavouring, as often as possible, to give "a local habitation and a name" to what has neither. Nowhere is this strange peculiarity of the uncultivated intellect perceived in a more tangible form than in the demonology of the Singhalese.

As may naturally be expected in such a system, created and

upheld merely by popular superstition, we find that not only are many of its tenets sometimes contrary to each other, but that the Cattadiyas (demon priests) and even the very books, which lay down the principles of their system, often differ from each other, so much so, indeed, that it is very difficult for any one, undertaking to give a connected and consistent account of the Demonism of Ceylon, to avoid sometimes making in one part of his account a statement inconsistent with another in another part of it. But as far as the Cattadiyas and their followers are themselves concerned, such difficulties are easily surmounted, by their attributing all such contradictions, if pointed out, to the mysteries of the art, and to their own ignorance, rather than to any fault of the system itself.

The Priests of Demonism are styled Yakaduras, Yakdessas, or more commonly, *Cattadiyas*; and there is scarcely a single village in the Island, which does not boast of at least one. Nearly twelve months are spent in learning the trade, the most laborious and principal part of the task of a beginner being, to commit to memory the charms, invocations, and songs, which are essential to his vocation. What the number of these is, may be estimated from the fact, that some of the demon-ceremonies commence at 6 or 7 P. M. and, lasting without intermission throughout the whole night, close only about 6 or 7, and sometimes later, the next morning; during all which time the performer has to repeat from memory all his charms and songs, only now and then interrupted by a violent bout of dancing. The dancing and the singing generally go on together, except when the former happens to be of so violent a nature, as to render it impossible to continue the other along with it. The profession was in early times exclusively confined to the low Castes, such as Tomtom Beaters, Durayas, and Jaggeries, but at present there is no such exclusiveness, men of every caste betaking themselves to it. The first man who ever practised the art, is said to have been one *Pradeys Rosia*.

A Cattadiya, who is a priest, though it be of demons, is yet never looked upon as in any way distinguished from the rest of the people by any supposed sanctity of character, or by a superior degree of intelligence; he wears no particular badge or dress like the Buddhist Priest, and receives no particular respect from any one ;—his ordinary life and avocations are like those of his neighbours; and as the members of his fraternity in the same village sometimes amount to three or four, his professional income does not suffice for his maintenance. He is therefore obliged to betake himself to some other supplementary business to increase his income. His profession is looked upon only as any ordinary calling, and commands no more respect than that of a boatman, a boutique keeper, a toddy drawer, or any other common trade. There is nothing of a sacred character belonging to it, as to that of the Buddhist Priests.

II. CAPUISM, like Demonism, also refers to the interests of this world; but while the object of the latter is to inflict or cure diseases by the agency of demons, the object of the former is to protect men generally against all manner of evil, and from diseases of a particular kind, such as small pox, chicken pox, and any epidemical disease of a malignant nature, and more especially to render prosperous the various avocations and trades of the people. The *dewiyo* or gods, who are the objects of worship in Capuism, are a more exalted class of beings, not possessed of the same evil dispositions as the demons, nor bringing like them sickness and death on innocent people; but reserving their powers of doing evil only for the punishment of those, who in any way displease them. But the punishment they inflict is always out of proportion to the nature of the offence. Although not so malignant as the demons, they are yet revengeful and irascible in their nature. They are more properly called *dewatawo* or inferior gods, and are propitiated by particular ceremonies. The priests of this worship are called *Capuas.* The priestesses of one of the principal goddesses belonging to this worship, named *Pattiny deviyo,* are called *Pattiny Hamies.* These Pattiny Hamies are not always females, males very often assuming the office. Both Pattiny Hamies and Capuas hold nearly the same rank in the estimation of their countrymen, and lead the same sort of life, as the Cattadiyas already mentioned; but in earlier days they were considered to be superior to the Cattadiyas, and in the inland districts of the Island they still retain this superiority to some extent. The sacred character however assigned to the Priests of Buddha is wholly denied both to the Capuas and to the Çattadiyas.

III. Grahaism, as it exists here at the present day, owes its origin to Judicial Astrology. The Horoscope of a man is an essential thing for determining both the nature of the planetary influence, which troubles him at any particular time with disease or some other evil, and also the nature of the particular ceremony necessary to remedy the evil. The calculations of the Astrologer shew that a certain position or a certain movement of the planets, or their arrival at a certain point of their orbit, is fraught with some calamity or some advantage to a man. When the former happens to be the case, the planet god, who is the cause of the evil, is propitiated by certain ceremonies called *Balli* ceremonies. These, being of various kinds, will come to be treated of in detail in a subsequent chapter. These Balli ceremonies have become more generally diffused through the Island since the reign of Sree Prakkrama Bahoo VI., who commenced his reign at Cottah in the year 1410, A. D. Before that time they were confined generally to the magnates of the land. When a king or a rich aristocrat fell sick, Brahmins and others skilled in the art were sent for from India, who sometimes also came of their own accord, and gave the benefit of their services only to those, who were able to pay them well: but Sreerahola Terunnanse, a Buddhist priest who lived during that reign, and who is reputed to have been the most learned man of his time in the Island, reduced Grahaism to its present condition, by teaching it to people of some of the low castes, and thereby rendering its benefits available to all classes of people. And so to this day, although every class of Singhalese engages in the worship, yet the office of priest or *Ballicaareya* or *Balleadura* is still held only by some of the low caste people, especially the *Berawayos* or Tomtom beaters.

CHAPTER II.

The Demons or Yakseyo.

The Demons or Yakseyo* are a class of beings forming a large community, under a government conducted by a King, and subject to laws enacted by him for their control, any infringement of which is followed by severe punishment. Wessamonny, this dreaded king, whose subjects throng every part of the sky, carries in his hand a sword of gold, of such wondrous power, that, when he is displeased with any of his subjects, it flies out of his hand of its own accord, and, after cutting off the heads of a thousand offenders with the rapidity of lightning, returns to his hand again. His laws are such as become the character of his subjects,—cruel, severe, and merciless, death being the rule, and any lighter penalty the exception in the punishment of any crime—burning, boiling, roasting, broiling, impaling, flaying alive, pouring melted metal down the

* Sir Emerson Tennent in his *Christianity in Ceylon* distinguishes *Yakseyos* from *Yakkas*, and describes the former as a gentle and benevolent race of beings, and the latter as malignant spirits; whereas, the truth is that both the terms, the former being the Sanscrit, and the latter the Singhalese word, mean the same thing. There are several other names by which these beings are known such as *Yakkha* (Pali), and *Yaksaya* (a Singhalese form of the Sanscrit term). The benevolent and gentle character, attributed by Sir Emerson, is true only of a portion of those Yakseyo mentioned in the Pali Buddhistical Works. But the malignant Yakseyo, who cause disease and suffering among men, are those who are worshipped in Demonism. These latter are not mentioned in the Buddhistical works, and are the indigenous demons of Ceylon, being creations of the popular fancy, existing in the belief of the Singhalese from a period perhaps long anterior to the introduction of Buddhism into the Island.

The *Rakseyo* are a race of beings, who differ from men only in being cannibals. They live solely on human flesh, which they obtain, not from graveyards or other places where human carcasses may be had, but by actually seizing and killing living men. They have no supernatural powers whatever like the Yakseyo. This notion about Rakseyo supports the idea that in the earliest periods of time this Island must have been inhabited by a race of men, who breakfasted on their fellowmen, like the inhabitants of some of the Polynesian Islands.

throat, driving sharp nails into the crown of the head, and a variety of other punishments, numbering 32 in all, distinguish his penal code. He has viceroys, ministers, and other officers necessary for the proper administration of his government. Between His Majesty and the mass of his subjects, there is a series of chiefs in regular gradation to each other, each of whom within his own allotted sphere of action exercises almost an unlimited amount of power. He exacts from all his subjects a degree of servile obedience to his will, which not the most despotic of earthly sovereigns ever pretended to claim; and the mere mention of his name is sufficient to make any of his subjects tremble with fear. His subjects spend their time almost always in amusing diversions of various kinds. Many of them at one time were so little under his rule that they openly attacked men, and either devoured them alive bones and all, or sucked their blood. Every Saturday and Wednesday, all the respectable demons attend a sort of pandemonium called *Yaksa Sabawa*, where each chieftain gives an account of the conduct of those under him to the principal chiefs; after which, they all engage in dancing, singing, playing on musical instruments, and in the display of exploits of skill and dexterity.

Demons are of two classes, those approaching to the nature of gods, wise, powerful, and not merciless, living in the upper regions of the sky, in magnificent palaces decorated with gold, silver, and precious stones, enjoying an amount of happiness little inferior to that of the gods themselves, and sometimes called *dewatawas;* and those, who with wild, savage, gross, beastly natures, pass their time near the surface of the earth, revelling in scenes of blood and misery, bringing disease and death on men, and receiving offerings of rice, meat, and blood, in return. The former class of demons are those mentioned in the Pali works, and do not belong to Demon-worship, but the latter, being those who are supposed to afflict men, are the objects of dread and of worship among the Singhalese.* These

* That none of the demons mentioned in the Buddhistical writings should be found to be objects of worship among the Singhalese, and that Demonism

are supposed to be the most terrible and hideous looking creatures in existence. Their aliment is blood and flesh, especially of human beings, but this not being allowed them now by their king, they are obliged to content themselves with making men sick, and accepting the offerings made by the sick people, which in imagination they suppose to be the flesh and blood of men, but do not, or cannot, actually eat; the only use they make of such offerings being to look at them, and enjoy the pleasure the sight affords them. By what other means they support existence, whether they take any kind of food whatever, or live by some supernatural means without the use of any food, neither the Cattadiya nor his books enable us to say.

They are said to have, in general, skins of a black colour, and large protruding eyes and hanging lips, with long white teeth, of which those called the canine, in some demons, project out of the mouth, curved like a pair of sickles. They sometimes wear about their persons venomous serpents, especially Cobras. They are invisible to men, but have the power of making themselves visible, generally in some other shape, often in that of beasts, of men or of women. As the favorite food of the cat is said to be rats, and that of tigers

---

recognizes demons wholly unknown to Buddhistical literature, do in themselves constitute a strong piece of internal evidence in proof of the greater antiquity of Demonism over Buddhism in this Island. For, had the latter been the one earlier established here, the probability, amounting almost to a certainty, is that the demons recognized by Buddhism itself would have been the demons who would have become objects of worship.

If Buddha and Wessamonny are mentioned in the invocations and charms of Demonism, as they often are, it only shews the natural result of two systems, which have continued to flourish together side by side for 2000 years and upwards, trying to adjust themselves to each other as much as possible: the more so when the believer in one system happens, as is the case here, to be also a believer in the other. Buddhism being considered to be the *sacred* religion, while Demonism is only a religion relating to one's temporal interests, it is natural that the influence of the former should to a certain extent be felt on the latter.

black cattle, so the favorite dish of a demon is said to be a living man. And because he is not allowed now to indulge himself in that luxury, he therefore takes pleasure in throwing his influence on men in a certain mysterious manner, which, it is said, is a source of enjoyment to him, as if he were actually engaged in sucking the blood out of some good looking man: it is also believed that this sort of enjoyment constitutes their only means of sustaining life, and that it is quite enough for the purpose. They are a sort of ubiquitous race, and yet have certain fixed residences in the north of the sky. They have the remarkable power of observing events which take place tens of thousands of miles remote from them, and can likewise travel millions of miles in a minute. The demons belonging to the first of these two classes are neither hideous as those of the second, nor do they eat men, nor even make men sick. In person they are like the gods themselves, with skins of golden hue. They use the ambrosial heavenly food used by the gods.

The second class of demons is subdivided into four minor divisions; viz., 1. *Balli-caama* demons, or those who have a particular attachment to balli offerings; 2. *Billi-caama* demons, or those fond of offerings of living beings; 3. *Ratti-caama* demons, or those who take delight in music, dancing, and other pleasures of that kind; 4. *Hantu-caama* demons, or those who delight in inflicting death. A disease brought on by a Hantu-caama demon is considered to be incurable by any means whatever; but those inflicted by the demons of the other three divisions terminate fatally, only when proper remedies are not applied, viz., those which Demonism affords.

In *Narayena*, the principal authority on the subject of the witchcraft, and to a certain extent of the demonology of India and the neighbouring countries, there appear the names of many demons, such as Asura Yakseya, Awara Yakseya, Heyma Yakseya, Peita Yakseya, Pralaapa Yakseya, Wayissrawana Yakseya, Kaksepa Yakseya, Nischella Yakseya, Gandarwa Yakseya, Naga Yakseya, and a great many others. But although Narayena is the received authority on the subject of charms among the Singhalese, yet none of these demons, mentioned in it as inflicting evils on men, are known to the Demonism of the Island. This circumstance is only another proof of the Demon-worship of the Singhalese having had an origin independent both of Brahminism or Hinduism, and of Buddhism.

According to Buddhism, neither *Brahmas** nor *Dewo* nor *Yakseyo* are born from the womb of a mother, but suddenly spring into existence full grown. This sort of birth is called *Oapapatika.* Nevertheless the last two classes, viz., Dewo and Yakseyo may have mothers in a peculiar fashion. For instance, if a demon seem to spring into existence from the shoulder or arm of a female demon, the latter is considered to be his mother. Marrying and giving in marriage prevail among them as well as among men. This is the account which Buddhism gives: but that given by Demonism itself differs very widely from this. It represents demons as having ***human*** fathers and mothers, and as being born in the ordinary course of nature. This is said to have been the case with almost every demon; but though born of human parents, all their qualities are different from those of men. They leave their parents sometime after their birth, but before doing so they generally take care to try

---

* Brahmas are the highest order of gods inhabiting the 16 highest heavens called *Brahma loka*, as the Dewo are the gods next below them in rank, inhabiting the 6 *Dewa loka* situated immediately below the former. Yakseyo are the demons. Brahmas are supposed seldom or never to interfere in the affairs of men, and are therefore never worshipped or invoked by the Singhalese; and even of the Dewo, the people worship only a few of the inferior classes, who do not even dwell in the 6 Dewa loka, but on the tops of large trees, and in the air above, not very far however from the earth, in magnificent palaces invisible to man. The Dewo of this latter class are called *dewata* generally, and are divided into *Tallatoo* and *Boomatoo* dewo. These are the dewo or gods that the people worship, as conferring benefits upon men or punishing them for their misdeeds. The more ignorant of the Singhalese Buddhists know no beings superior to these. These inferior gods are partly Hindoo deities, and partly deified heroes of the Singhalese.

The fact of Brahmas being mentioned by Buddha as the highest class of beings in existence, inferior only to himself, inhabiting 16 lokas or worlds, is an additional, though a collateral, proof of Brahminism being anterior to Buddhism.

their demoniac powers on them. In the first place they must pay their court to Wissamonny, or to some powerful god, and obtain from him permission to exercise their demoniac powers. They then hover about in the air, and cease to touch the ground; for walking on the ground is strictly prohibited by Wissamonny and the gods; nevertheless, whenever a man says that he has seen the apparition of a demon, he always describes him as having appeared to him walking on the ground like a man.

It also appears in the various accounts given of the birth of demons, especially in the genealogical accounts recited or chanted at the commencement of demon ceremonies, that a demon has the power at any moment (a power which he often exercises) of entering the womb of a woman, where he remains during the necessary period, assuming in their order the various conditions of a foetus conceived in the ordinary way. After the woman's delivery, the child (that is the demon) resumes the exercise of his demon peculiarities, as before. Some demons appear to have been born hundreds of times in this fashion.

If we can believe that there is any particle of truth at all in the existence and in the genealogies of these demons, that little, we think, must be this—that in the very remotest periods, when the Singhalese were peculiarly ignorant and superstitious, and when the principle of Hero-worship was carried to a height proportioned only to the ignorance of the worshipper, there may have lived particular members of the community, who distinguished themselves by extreme ferocity and cruelty of conduct, joined to considerable power, which they exercised either as kings, chiefs, or mere lawless freebooters; and that these individuals after death, and perhaps when living, were worshipped as supernatural beings possessed of irresistible powers of injuring men. We are the more confirmed in this opinion by the fact, that the dewo or gods belonging to Capuism appear to have been no more than creatures of this kind. The mythology and the apotheosis of the Greeks, of the Romans and of most other early nations of the world were, in a manner, only counterparts of this.

There is another class of demons who come into existence by *Oapapatika* birth. These are called *Malla Yakseyo,* or the spirits of deceased men. If a man, who lives at enmity with another, remember, on his deathbed, just before he dies, and at the very moment of his expiring, any thing relating to that enmity, and if, instead of a feeling of forgiveness, resentment and hatred take possession of his mind, he is supposed to become, after death, a demon of this kind. These demons are not so powerful, as those mentioned above, nevertheless they too cause sickness.

There are two places distinguished as the birthplaces of many of the demons. These are *Wisala Maha Newera* (Ujayin), and *Sanka paala Newera.* These cities are said to have, on very many occasions, been laid desolate by demons, either by inflicting disease upon the citizens or by devouring them alive.

To shew the reader that the notion of the possibility of a human mother giving birth to a demon even in these days, is not at all uncommon among the people, we have only to mention an incident which is still fresh in our recollection. A poor woman of our native village gave birth to a child about 23 or 24 years ago; the infant, which was a male, had all its teeth as well developed, as a child of 5 or 6 years of age. Its head too was covered with hair about an inch long, its face was unusually long, and its mouth broader than usual in children of that age. The appearance of the child was not at all prepossessing, and all thought that it was a demon. An hour or two after its birth the grandfather dashed out its brains with a stick. To this day, the people believe that it was actually a demon and not a human being, and this belief will, we are sure, continue for centuries more. On our mentioning this circumstance some years ago, to an English gentleman now high in the Civil Service of this Island, he gave information of it to Government, who in consequence instructed the local magistrate to make an investigation into the matter. But those of the villagers, who were well acquainted with the particulars of the case, considering it more prudent to hold their tongues, than to give information in a matter, in which they were not personally interested, denied all knowledge of it.

Another child was also sacrificed to this same superstition about 25 years ago in a village near Barberyn. In this case, the child was nailed to the stem of a cocoanut tree and so left to die, the best punishment, as was thought, for a demon, who had had the impudence to be born of a human mother. We have also heard of a still more recent case, which occurred some 5 or 6 years ago in the same neighbourhood, but we are not acquainted with any of the particulars connected with it. We have likewise heard of 10 or 12 other cases of this kind, which have occurred within the last 25 years in other parts of the Island, in which ignorance and superstition triumphed both over parental affection and over common sense.

The demons can never inflict disease or receive offerings, unless they have a sort of general permission called *Wurrun*, previously granted to them by Wissamonny, or by some of his principal chiefs, or by some of the gods. And as they cannot *honestly* sustain life without afflicting men, and thereby extorting offerings, they are necessarily obliged to seek and obtain this *Wurrun*, as soon as they enter on life. Inferior and insignificant demons however live on without such a patent, by violating the law, and their sufferings and punishments are therefore very great. The principal offenders of this kind are the demons called *Malla Yakseyo.*

Like men, demons also seem to have their own fashionable hours of breakfasting, dining, and supping. *Sanny Yakseya* will accept his offerings only in the morning between 2 and 6 o'clock; *Reeri Yakseya, Calloo Yakseya, Abimaana Yakseya,* and *Totte Yakseya,* will accept their's only in the evening, between 6 and 10 o'clock; while *Maha Sohon Yakseya, Hooniyan Yakseya, Uda Yakseya,* the female demons *Riddhi Yaksaniya* and *Madana Yakseniya* will accept offerings at no other hours than those intervening between 10 P. M., and 2 A. M.

Although it is believed that there are millions and billions of demons in existence, yet the number of those who belong to the demon worship does not exceed 50 or 60, and even of these Reeri Yakseya, Calloo Yakseya, Sanny Yakseya, Maha Sohon Yakseya, Calloo Cumare dewatawa, and Hooniyan Yakseya, are the principal individuals, who figure in every demon ceremony in the Island.

I. REERI YAKSEYA or REERI YAKKA* (demon of blood) is considered to be the most cruel and powerful of all these. He is represented as having the face of a monkey, and the rest of his body like that of a man. The colour of his skin is a fiery red. He uses a red bull to ride on. There is scarcely a single disease, to which a Singhalese man is liable, in which this demon is not supposed to exert an influence. Diseases, which produce a flux of blood from the system, are supposed to be especially inflicted by him. When a man is about to die, this demon is supposed to be present by means of an *avatar*† or apparition called *Maru Avatar*, or apparition of death. On such an occasion he is supposed to assume the dimensions of a pigmy, measuring one span and six inches in height, and carrying in one hand a cock, in the other a club, and in his mouth the corpse of a man; he is supposed to be present at the death bed, or not far off, till the man dies. Every demon, as well as Reeri Yakseya, has several forms of these apparitions or disguises, which he assumes on different occasions according to circumstances, and in each of which he is called by a different name. There is however another opinion entertained by some of the Cattadiyas, that these apparitions are not different disguises of the same demon, but that they are separate individual demons, forming however a sort of confederacy, and all acting together in concert. The former, we think, is the more popular opinion of the two. Nevertheless, in the case of one demon, viz., Sanni Yakseya, these apparitions are sup-

* Yakseya and Yakka are synonymous terms, of which the latter however is the one which is more commonly used.

† *Avatar* is a Sanscrit term signifying the incarnation of any being or spirit in some particular shape. Among the Hindoos an avatar of being, such, for instance, as that of Vishnoo, is some condition of existence, such as that of a cow, a man, a serpent or some other, which Vishnoo chooses to assume or to be born in. An *avatar* of a demon, as understood amongst the Singhalese, means some disguise which a demon assumes for a few moments or so. It is also supposed that the demon himself is not bodily present at any place where such an avatar is seen, but that he is millions of miles distant from the scene, and yet has the power of creating these avatars and of presenting them to the eyes of men.

posed to be not his own disguised self, but separate individual demons, who act under him and in obedience to his orders. Reeri Yakseya has 18 of these apparitions, or avatars as they are called by the people. In the 1st he is called *Reeri Yakseya;* in the 2nd *Ree Raj-ja;* 3rd *Agu Raj-ja;* 4th *Pulutajja;* 5th *Reeri Gopolla;* 6th *Reeri Buddia;* 7th *Reeri Watukaya;* 8th *Reeri Billey Dewatawa;* 9th *Reeri Kavisia;* 10th *Reeri Sanniya;* 11th *Reeri Curumberaya;* 12th *Reeri Madana Yakseya;* 13th *Lay Avatar Yakseya;* 14th *Lay Caama Yakseya;* 15th *Serra Marulu Dewatawa;* 16th *Maru Reeri Yakseya;* 17th *Maru Caama Yakseya;* and in the 18th *Maru Avatar Yakseya.* Reeri Yakseya is represented to have had above a hundred different incarnations; in one of which he was the son of a king of Sanka pala Nuwera; in another, of a king of Lagal pura; in a third, of a she-demon named Ginimuru Yaksani of a country called Hanumanta Desay; but his disposition and conduct were the same in all.

II. Maha Sohon Yakseya, or Maha Sohona means the *Great Graveyard Demon.* He is so named because he chiefly frequents graveyards. He is also supposed to haunt the summits of large rocks and hills, where he delights to surround himself with human carcasses, and to swallow huge morsels of the delicious repast, preferring the entrails above all other parts. He is 81 cubits (122 feet) high; has three eyes, four hands, and a skin of a red colour. His origin is thus given—"In ancient times, there were giants in this Island, men who could defeat even half a dozen elephants in single combat by their mere physical strength. One of these giants, by name *Jaya Sena,* was very fond of displaying his extraordinary strength, even at times when there was no occasion for it, and happening on one occasion to pick a quarrel with *Gota Imbra,* another great giant, the latter with one blow knocked off his head. Precisely at that moment the planet god *Senasura,* who was a spectator of the scene, seized a bear, and tearing off its head from its body, applied it to the headless trunk of Jaya Sena, to which through his supernatural power it adhered, and became a part of the body. So the deceased Jaya Sena instantly rose up alive as a demon, and has since been known as *Maha Sohona* in reference to his habits of haunting graveyards."* In those demon ceremonies, which are performed to obtain the release of a sick man from the influence of Maha Sohona, a certain spell or charm called *Gota Imbra Dæhænay* is made use of by the Cattadiya. In this charm the particulars of this event are narrated at length, and the demon is threatened with further vengeance from his late conqueror, if he does not afford immediate relief to the sufferer. Maha Sohona is the chief of 30,000 demons. He also shews himself to men in various disguises or apparitions when he moves about, and on each occasion rides on a particular animal. In one of these apparitions he rides on a goat, and is called *Lay Sohona* or *Blood Demon of the graveyard;* in another he rides on a deer, and is named *Amu Sohona* or the *graveyard Demon of fresh corpses;* in a third he rides on a horse, and is called *Jaya Sohona,* or the *Victorious demon of the graveyard;* in a fourth he rides on a sheep, and is called *Maru Sohona* or the *graveyard demon of death;* in a fifth he rides on an elephant, and is called *Golu Sohona* or the *Dumb demon of the graveyard;* In his own proper person as *Maha Sohona* he rides on a gigantic hog.

---

* The *graveyards* of ancient times in Southern Asia, and especially in Ceylon, were not what we commonly understand by that term now. Excepting the Buddhist priests and the aristocrats of the land, whose bodies were burnt in regular funeral piles after death, the corpses of the rest of the people were neither burned nor buried, but thrown into a place called *Sohona*, which was an open piece of ground in the jungle, generally a hollow among the hills, at the distance of 3 or 4 miles from any inhabited place, where the corpses were left in the open air to be decomposed, or devoured by dogs and wild beasts. This practice appears to have prevailed in the Island to a comparatively recent period, and in the most secluded and least civilized of the inland districts till about the beginning of this century. Although regular cemeteries are mentioned in the *Maha Wanso* in connection with Anuradhapura, especially during the reign of the Wijeyan dynasty, they do not appear to have been very general either at that time or at any subsequent period. Maha Sohona and other demons not having now these *(Sohon)* congenial places for demoniac conviviality, are obliged to be content with the ordinary graves and graveyards of these days.

III. MAHA COLA SANNI YAKSEYA, or the *Great Demon of the fatal diseases,* according to one account, sprang into existence from the ashes of the funeral pile of *Asoopala Cumari,* a princess of the city *Wisala Maha Nuwera.** Another account makes him the son of a king of a city, called *Sanka pala Nuwera.* † "This king," says the account, during the pregnancy of his queen, made an incursion into the country in search of some article of *Dolladuk* for her, ‡ and, on returning to his palace a few days afterwards, one of the queen's servants, who was unfriendly to her,

* "Wisala," says Professor Wilson, "is a city of considerable renown in Indian tradition, but its site is a subject of some uncertainty. Part of the difficulty arises from confounding it with Visala, another name of Ujayin. According to the Buddhists, it is the same as Prayaga or Allahabad; but the Ramayana places it much lower down, on the north Bank of the Ganges, nearly opposite to the mouth of the Sone; and it was therefore in the modern district of Saran, as Hamilton (Genealogy of the Hindus) conjectured."—*Wilson's Vishnu Purana.*

Fa Hian visited Wisala, but does not give any extended description of what he saw. Hiuen Thsang is more particular, and says that it had fallen into ruin, but that the circumference of the ancient foundations was upwards of twenty miles. He saw the ruins of more than a hundred monasteries. The country was rich, the soil fertile, the climate agreeable, and the inhabitants were bland in their manners, and contended with their lot. There were a few monasteries still standing, but the inmates were little better than heretics."—*Hardy's Manual of Buddhism.*

There is scarcely any other place more frequently alluded to in the demonology of Ceylon, than this city, which in Singhalese is generally known under the name of *Wisala Maha Nuware* which means the "great extensive city."

† Sometimes also, called *Sakaspura,* and in Pali *Sankassa.* "A letter from Lieutenant Cunningham, R. E., to Colonel Sykes, was read before the Royal Asiatic Society, December 3, 1842, giving an account of the discovery and identification of the city of Sankasya mentioned as the kingdom of Kusadwaga in the Ramayana. It is twenty-five miles from Farrkhabad, and fifty from Kanouj on the north or left bank of the Kali Nadi. The ruins are very extensive, and there can be no doubt that they are of Buddhistic origin"—*Hardy's Manual of Buddhism.*

‡ *Dolladuk* is a strong desire which a woman during the earlier months of her pregnancy has for something, generally some article of food. This desire

wishing to ruin her, told the king that she was unfaithful to his bed. On this, the injured king ordered her to be put to death. Her body was to be cut into two pieces, of which one was to be hung upon an *Ukberiya* tree, and the other to be thrown at its foot to be devoured by dogs. When the queen heard of this, she was enraged beyond measure, because she knew that she was wholly innocent. So she said, 'if this charge be false, may the child in my womb be born this instant a demon, and may that demon destroy the whole of this city with its unjust king.' No sooner had the king's executioners done as they were ordered, than the half of the corpse, which was suspended on the tree, falling down on the ground, united itself to the other half which was at the foot of the tree; and the same instant the corpse gave birth to a demon, who first sucked his mother's breasts, then sucked her blood, and lastly devoured her, flesh and bones. He then went to the Sohon graveyards in the vicinity, and there lived upon the carcasses. Afterwards repairing to the city and inflicting a mortal disease on the king, he began with several other demons, who now formed his retinue, to devour the citizens, and in a short time nearly depopulated the city. The gods Iswara and Sekkra, seeing the ferocity of this new demon, came down to the city, disguised as mendicants, and after some little resistance on the part of the demon, they subdued him; on which occasion they ordered him to abstain from eating men, but gave him Wurrun or permission to inflict disease on mankind, and to obtain offerings from them. According to some

---

is often an irresistible one. Sometimes it happens to be a very unreasonable one too. We know a woman still living, who, when in this interesting condition about 15 or 20 years ago, expressed a strong wish to eat the head of a little child, and her husband was able to moderate her cannibal propensity, only by substituting the heads of fishes and other animals for that of a child. The husband and all her relatives and neighbours suspected that such a desire could not but be a prelude to the birth of a demon, and accordingly awaited the event with much anxiety and curiosity. Happily, however, the child did not happen to have long teeth or long hair, and so had the good fortune to escape the fate which it would have otherwise met with.

accounts this demon has 4,448, and according to others 484,000 subject demons under him. He generally rides on a lion, and has 18 principal attendants, the first of whom is called *Bhoota Sanni Yakseya*, or the *demon of madness;* 2nd *Maru Sanni Yakseya*, or the *demon of death;* 3rd *Jala Sanni Yakseya*, or the *demon of cholera;* 4th *Wewulun Sanni Yakseya*, or the *demon of cold and trembling fits;* 5th *Naga Sanni Yakseya*, or the *demon of a disease resembling that from the sting of a Cobra de Capello;* 6th *Gana Sanni Yakseya*, or the *demon of blindness;* 7th *Corra Sanni Yakseya*, or the *demon of lameness;* 8th *Gollu Sanni Yakseya*, or the *demon of dumbness;* 9th *Bihiri Sanni Yakseya*, or the *demon of deafness;* 10th *Wata Sanni Yakseya*, or the *demon of diseases caused by the wind;* 11th *Pit Sanni Yakseya*, or the *demon of bilious diseases;* 12th *Sen Sanni Yakseya*, or the *demon of diseases influenced by the phlegm;** 13th *Demala Sanni Yakseya*, or the *Tamil demon of diseases;* 14th *Murtu Sanni Yakseya*, or the *demon of fainting fits and swoons;* 15th *Arda Sanni Yakseya*, or the *demon of Apoplexy;* 16th *Wedi Sanni Yakseya*, or the *demon of a disease which kills one instantly like a shot from a gun;* 17th *Dewa Sanni Yakseya*, or the *demon of diseases influenced by the gods;* and 18th *Aturu Sanni Yakseya*, or the servant of Maha Cola Sanni Yakseya (the chief of all the 18.) These 18 demons are not considered to be mere apparitions of the same demon, as in the case of the other Yakseyo, but separate individual demons acting together in concert with their chief Maha Cola Sanni Yakseya.

IV. Oddy Cumara Hooniyan Dewatawa † is the son of *Susiri*, queen of *Sagalpura* in *Maduratta*. He always rides on

* *Wind, phlegm* and *bile* are considered by the Singhalese physicians to be the proximate causes of every sickness, to which man is liable: and in the treatment of any disease, one or more of these three agents have to be influenced.

† Though *dewatawa* is a term, which is generally applied to the inferior classes of gods, and to the superior classes of demons, that do not inflict disease on men, yet it is also sometimes applied by Cattadiyas, as in the text, to inferior or malignant demons.

a horse. He has six different apparitions; in the first he is called *Cala Oddisey*, or *demon of incurable diseases;* in the second *Naga Oddisey*, or *demon of serpents;* in the third *Cumara Oddisey*, or *demon prince;* in the fourth *Demala Oddisey*, or *Tamil demon*; in the fifth *Gopolu Oddisey*, or *demon of Cattle;* and in the sixth *Raja Oddisey*, or *Royal demon.* He is the principal demon that has much to do in that department of sorcery called *Hooniyan.**

V. Calu Yakseya, or the *Black Demon*, is so named on account of the extremely black colour of his skin. He appears in four different apparitions; in the first he is called *Calu Curumbera*, or the *blackest one;* in the second, *Rata Calu Yakseya*, or the *foreign black demon;* in the third, *Dewol Bagey Calu Yakseya*, or the *Black demon of the Dewol gods;* and in the fourth *Siddhi Calu Yakseya*, or the *Illustrious black demon.* He was generated from the ashes of the burnt corpse of Basma, an Asura.† Another account makes him a son of king Wijeyo by Cuveni. A third account says that he is the spirit of a famous giant named *Neela Maha Yodaya*, who formed one of the bodyguard of king *Gaja Bahu* (113 A. D.) He once accompanied the king on a visit to a country called *Istreepura*, which was inhabited only by females (a race of Amazons), all of whom on seeing him fell in love with him. Hundreds of them seizing him at once, each claiming him as her own, and pulling him this way and that way, he was torn to pieces in their grasp. His spirit having assumed the form of a

* It is not now easy to identify the *Sagalpura* mentioned in the text. Many believe it to be the *Sagal* of King Milinda, who is celebrated for his controversies with Nagesena; but this opinion is hardly tenable, when we consider that the capital of Milinda must have been somewhere in or near Cashmere, and that Messrs. Wilson, Bird, and Masson, consider it to have been situated between the rivers Ravi and Pipasa in the Punjab; while the Sagal of the text is expressly mentioned as being in Maduratta, which is on the opposite side of India.

† *Asuras* are a race of beings of enormous size, supposed to reside under the mythical rock *Maha Meru*. They are the Titans of Singhalese mythology.

Demon is now always trying to avenge his wrongs on the whole female sex. Women and little children are therefore supposed to suffer from his malign influence.

VI. Calu Cumara Dewatawa or the *Black Prince* is the son of king Boksella and his queen Sonalu. He shews himself to men in seven different apparitions: in the 1st he is called *Handung Cumara*, or *Prince of sandal perfumes;** in the 2nd *Andung Cumara*, or Prince of *Eye Ointments;*† in the 3rd *Mal Cumara*, or *Prince of flowers;* in the 4th *Gini Cumara*, or *Prince of fire;* in the 5th *Dala Cumara*, or the *Rough Prince;* in the 6th *Sohon Cumara*, or *Prince of graves;* and in the 7th *Wala Cumara*, or

---

*There is scarcely a single offering made to any demon in which *Sandal wood* does not form a constituent part: and Demon worship, be it remembered, is a system, which seems to have prevailed here from times anterior to those of Wijeyo himself. This circumstance, taken together with the fact, that the Chinese writers actually mention Sandal wood as forming in early times an article of export from this Island, seems to favor the idea, that the article must have been growing in the Island in considerable quantities in early times, though at present specimens are to be met with only in a few spots, and those preserved rather as objects of curiosity and ornament than for use.

†The *soot*, which is produced on a piece of porcelain when held to the lighted wick of a lamp, is scraped up and mixed with a little cocoanut oil, when it acquires the name *andung* or Eye Ointment, so called because it is rubbed on the outside of the eyelids of very young infants by Singhalese mothers, who believe it to be productive of some benefit to the eyes. Can it be that this benefit is the protecting of the tender eyes of the young infant from being dazzled by too much light, that the black pigment is laid all round the cornea of the eye in order that it may imbibe all the straggling rays of light which, falling on the parts nearest to the cornea, by reflection, tend to injure the tender retina by an overabundance of light? If this be the case, it will warrant the supposition, that the Singhalese were *practically* acquainted with the Theory of Light, tens of centuries before Newton was born. The practice is one of the most ancient among the Singhalese.

This Eye Ointment also forms an important item in the offerings made to demons in many demon ceremonies: but for what use it is intended to serve a demon it is difficult to guess. In a certain ceremony performed to propitiate the demon *Calu Cumara dewatawa*, the Cattadiya, who performs the ceremony, paints his eyelids with this Ointment.

Prince of a smooth body. He is always tormented by the passion of love, and when his evil influence falls upon females, it is supposed to make them ill. Young and fair women are particularly exposed to his attacks. Another account says that he was the son of a king, and that afterwards on taking orders as a Buddhist priest his piety and sanctity of life became so great, that, besides other superhuman powers, he acquired that of flying through the air like a bird, but that on a certain occasion, while so moving in the air, seeing the beautiful daughter of a certain king of India, he was so much struck with her beauty, that he fell in love, and losing at the same time all his supernatural powers dropped down on the very spot, where the object of his passion was standing at the time. His passion was so intense, that it broke his heart, and he died on the spot, and became a demon, since called Calu Cumara Dewatawa. He is considered to be a demon of great respectability, more civilized and less savage than the rest of his fraternity. Great care is therefore taken in the preparation of his offerings. Rice of the best quality and cooked in the best manner, the best kinds of plantains, sugar canes, oranges, king-cocoanuts, sugar, and several varieties of cakes, constitute the principal articles in the offerings made to him. His person is of a dark blue colour, and his garments of a deep black.

VII. Ahimana Yakseya was born of an *Aandy** woman. His father was a king of Gururatta in Casee-dayse. He is known under three other names, *Ollala Yakseya*, *Malala Yakseya*, and *Cotta Yakseya* or *short demon*, so called in reference to the short stumps of his legs, which were cut off in a battle fought with king Wijeyo.

VIII. Tota Yakseya, son of king *Malala* and his queen *Sandagana* of the city of *Sandagana Nuvera*, passes most of his time at the ferries and fords of rivers; and it is at these places that he casts his influence on men.

---

* *Aandy* is the name of a class of Moormen, whose sole pursuits are begging and fortune-telling. They are the Gypsies of Ceylon. Their language, religion, and dress are the same as those of the Moormen, but still it is open to doubt whether they are of the same race.

IX. Bahirawa Yakseya is another demon as much attached to the female sex as *Calu Cumara dewatawa* himself, but there is this difference between them:—while the latter brings only slight diseases on the objects of his attachment, the former inflicts those that result in speedy death. The hill called *Bahirawa Canda*, which stands towering like a giant over one side of the town of Kandy, was till very lately supposed to be the abode of this demon. In early days it was regarded with feelings of dread. One of the former kings of Kandy, seeing that he was not likely to have any issue to perpetuate his line on the thorne, his queen miscarrying within a few months of her confinement whenever she was pregnant, assembled all the astrologers, soothsayers, cattadiyas, and other men of similar crafts, to his palace, and on consulting them as to the cause of his misfortune, was told, that the queen was under the influence of the demon Bahirawa Yakseya, who would never remove his influence from her, unless a yearly sacrifice of a young virgin was made to him on the summit of Bahirawa Canda. The king did as he was directed, and it is said that, after that, he had several children born to him. But when his queen grew old and past the time of child-bearing, he discontinued the offering as unnecessary, on which, it is said, the displeased demon began to inflict diseases on the royal family and on all the citizens, in so much that within two months the city was nearly depopulated. By the advice of his ministers and the Cattadiyas, the king resumed the former practice of making the annual sacrifice, to which all his successors, till the very last, faithfully adhered. The sacrifice was performed at night in the following manner:—A stake being driven into the ground on the summit of the hill, the girl was tied to it with jungle creepers; flowers and boiled rice were placed close by on an altar constructed for the purpose; certain invocations and incantations were then pronounced, which completed the ceremony. The next morning the girl was found dead; and no wonder, for it would be a miracle, if a Singhalese, especially a young female destined to propitiate a demon, left alone for a night on the top of a hill supposed to be haunted, and tied to a stake, with the sound of the terrible charms still ringing in her ears, did not die through fright within an hour. There is, however, an old woman still living in Kandy, who was so offered up to the demon, in the time of the last king, Sree Wickrama Raja Singha, but who somehow or other managed to effect her escape. Besides this annual offering, there were others of a less important character, made 3 or 4 times every year to the demon on the same hill. There are seven other demons also known by the same name Bahirawa, but all the eight form a sort of company. When at Kandy on Circuit with the Supreme Court, I twice ascended the hill, and stood on its summit on the very spot, on which I thought the fatal stake must have been fixed. The summit is a small level area, not more than 20 or 25 feet square. Although the demon is said to have left the mountain soon after the British took possession of Kandy in 1815, yet even now few Singhalese have the hardihood to go to its summit alone at night, especially on a Saturday or a Wednesday night.

X. MADANA YAKSENIYO, or *Female demons of Lust*, is the common name of seven sisters, namely *Cama Madana*, or *demon of Lust;* 2 *Cini Madana*, or *demon of fire;* 3 *Mohanee Madana*, or *demon of ignorance;* 4 *Ratti Madana*, or *demon of pleasure;* 5 *Cala Madana*, or *demon of maturity;* 6 *Mal Madana*, or *demon of flowers;* and 7 *Puspa Madana*, or *demon of Perfumes.* These demons, when worked upon by certain charms, and propitiated with certain offerings and ceremonies, are supposed to use their power of seducing the affections of a man or a woman in such a manner, that the person so influenced is said to find the power perfectly irresistible. There are hundreds of ways, in which it is pretended that this can be done; among others, by touching the person of a female with the young leaf of a king cocoanut tree, previously subjected to the incantations and other ceremonies peculiar to the mysteries of the art; by the man rubbing on his face a charmed medicine and then shewing himself to her; by mixing some love potion, similarly charmed, with her food; by making her chew charmed beetle leaves; by carrying on his person a charmed thread previously taken from a cloth she had worn; or by any of a hundred other ways, in all of which the Madana Yakseniyo become useful agents in the hands of the magician. But the most efficacious and unfailing of all these methods is considered to be a certain oil called *Madana Tayiley*, a single drop of which, sprinkled on the person of a female, is supposed to act irresistibly on her: but the preparation of the wonderful oil is said to be fraught with so much danger to those engaged in it, that few or none dare to attempt it, and those who do, seldom or never succeed, as the demons are supposed to do their best to disappoint the men by frightening and scaring them away from the scene of their operations, which is said to result in the incurable insanity and eventual or immediate death of the operators.

A short time ago we found the inhabitants of our native village in a high state of excitement, owing to the freaks that a mad man was playing in the neighbourhood. It was said that he had become a maniac by attempting to make the oil Madane Tayiley; that he had, for the last few days, been living in the woods eating serpents, frogs, and other loathsome creatures; that he stirred out in the darkness of the night with no other clothing on his person than a few green *Gurulla* leaves* tied round his waist; that he carried in his hands a man's skull and a bone, and on his shoulders a pot of human blood, which he used to slake his thirst; and that his favorite sleeping places were graves. For three or four days together nothing else was talked of in the village. By and bye the real truth eked out from other sources, but not from the villagers themselves. It appeared that a mad man, a native of Salpitty Corle, breaking loose from his keepers, had wandered about from village to village, and that during these wanderings he happened one night to pass through the villages we have alluded to above, accompanied

---

* *Gurulla* or *Burulla* is a kind of plant, between which and the demons there smees to be some mysterious connection. It is used in the construction and decoration of the altars and other structures, which are made in many of the Demon ceremonies. The Cattadiya sometimes adorns his head and his waist with its leaves in certain ceremonies.

by a relative, who had come to take him home, and that this relative was the first to tell one of the villagers of the cause of the madness. By the next morning the report had spread through the village like wildfire, magnified and ornamented with the additions we have given above. The villagers themselves were, however, loth to believe the truth, when we told it to them, denuded of the additions they had made to it. The relative of the madman told us, a few days afterwards, the cause of the madman's misfortune; he described to us, how the man had endeavoured to make Madana Tayiley, about a year ago, and had been frightened by demons just at the moment of the oil becoming perfected, and how he, in consequence, had become a maniac. Although Madana Yakseniyo and their wonderful oil are matters, about which we and this relative of the madman essentially differ in opinion from each other, yet, as to the mere fact of the man having become mad on such an occasion, we do not differ at all; for considering the extent of superstitious fear, which is ever present in the mind of an ignorant Singhalese, and especially on such an occasion, as that of preparing the oil of the demons, in the dead of night, on a lonesome grave, in a lonely part of the village, and his belief in the presence, at the scene of his operations, of cruel and powerful demons, whom he himself has but just invoked, and that these demons are ready at any unguarded moment, during the process of making the oil, to pounce upon him and destroy him and his oil—when we consider these things, it is not at all improbable that a Singhalese, through mere excess of fright and an overexcited imagination, should lose his reason and become a maniac.

XI. MOROTTOO YAKA, or *Demon of Morottoo*, or *Rata Yaka* or *Foreign demon*, is so named from his being a foreigner who landed at Morottoo, when he first came over into this country from the Malabar Coast. Soon after his landing, he fixed his residence on the top of a large tree in the neighbourhood of Morottoo, and whilst living there he brought so much sickness upon men, and especially upon children and women in a state of pregnancy, that the whole district was said to have been filled with mourning during every part of the year. For a long time he continued to exercise his malignant power, till on one occasion he brought sickness on the queen of Sree Prakkrama Bahu VI., king of Cottah, which was then called Jayawardanapura (1410 A. D.) When the king found, that the medicines of the most skilful physicians of his *Gabadawa*, or Royal College of Physicians, were of no avail, he consulted the most learned men of his kingdom as to the cause of the Queen's illness, and learned from them that it was caused by *Morottoo Yaka.* Only one Cattadiya however in all his kingdom knew the ceremony, by which the demon could be appeased. That ceremony called *Rata Yakum Neteema*, or *Morottoo Yakum Neteema*, was accordingly performed, and the royal lady was restored to health.

XII. GOPOLU YAKSEYA, or the *Demon of cattle*, was the son of a king or chief of a district on the Coromandel Coast. He was the twinbrother of *Mangara Dewiyo* (a demigod;) their mother having died soon after their birth, a cow-buffalo suckled them: but Gopolu having on one occasion sucked all the milk without leaving any for his brother, a quarrel ensued, in which Gopolu was killed, but being born again, as the nature of demons is, he came over to Ceylon, and landed at Arangodde near Katragamma. At Arangodde he lived on a Banyan tree in which there was a large beehive, and scattered disease and death among all who came near the tree. His old enemy Mangara dewiyo and *Pattini dewiyo* (goddess of chastity) came afterwards to Ceylon, and, happening to land at the same place, saw a number of men lying under the tree, some dead and others dying. Knowing the cause, they immediately ordered the neighbouring villagers to bring a cow-buffalo, which they ordered to be offered up in sacrifice to Gopolu, on which the dying men recovered and returned to their houses. He is called the demon of cattle, because all cattle sickness is supposed to proceed from him. He is also considered to be the cause of hydrophobia.

XIII. ANJENAM DEWI is a female demon, by whose aid a certain art of divination called here *Anjenam beleema*, and elsewhere, as in Egypt, *divining by the Magic Mirror*, is performed. She is the chief of 700 other female demons.

XIV. BADDRACALI, is a female demon, whose assistance is sought for winning lawsuits, and for subduing enemies and rivals of any kind.

XV. RIDDHI YAKSENIYO are seven female demons, who also bring disease on men, like any other demons.

XVI. UDA YAKSEYO. There are many demons of this name. They are as cruel, as any of the preceding.

XVII. CURUMBERA YAKSEYO. Of this name also there are several, all equally prodigal of their powers of inflicting sickness.

XVIII. HANUMA is another powerful demon of great cruelty.

These are the principal demons, who figure in Demon Ceremonies, either as having caused disease, or as the effective agents in curing it. But there are also a very large number of demons of inferior power, collectively called *Mala Yakseyo,* who also inflict diseases of a less malignant character. These demons, as mentioned in a preceding page, are, as their name implies, the spirits of deceased men, born as demons in consequence of some demerit of theirs when living as men, or of some feeling of animosity or hatred, which was uppermost in their thoughts at the moment of death.

In addition to both these classes of demons, there is a third, which includes a few demons of a different kind. These are *Gara Yaka, Dewalla Yakseya,** *Bodrima,* and the *Pretayo.*

XIX. GARA YAKA has no evil disposition, like those already described. He does no harm whatever to men, but on the contrary assists them in expelling all sorts of evil influence, to which new houses are supposed to be subject. Hence, when a house has been built, before or soon after its occupation, a ceremony called *Gara Yaka Maduwa* is generally performed, without which it is supposed that some misfortune will fall upon the inmates. Gara Yakseya is represented to be an individual of a voracious appetite and a capacious stomach. On one occasion *Pattini Dewiyo,* the goddess

---

* *Yaka* and *Yakseya* are synonymous terms, both equally used by the Singhalese. The first is derived from the Pali *Yakkho,* and the second from the Sanscrit *Yaksha.*

of chastity, having to accompany the wedding procession of *Canda Cumara* (the god of Kattragam), but not wishing to do so, because the house, together with all the furniture prepared for the reception of the guests, was wholly constructed of the bones and skins of animals (the adopted father of the bride happening to be a Weddah), she ordered Gara Yakseya to go there in time, and see what he could do before her arrival. Accordingly he went to the house in the character of *Gamana*,* and not seeing any better way of clearing the house of its disagreeable furniture, at once fell to devouring every thing, and in a short time the whole building with all its furniture was deposited in his stomach; to show his host, that hedid this merely to satisfy his hunger, and not for any other purpose, he, even after this feat of gastronomic power, said that he was still very hungry. Before he commenced to eat the house, he had also eaten all the food, that had been prepared for the whole wedding party. Lastly, to satisfy his thirst, he drank some thousands of young Cocoanuts, and then drank up all the wells in the neighbourhood: and after all this, he left the house in great displeasure, saying to his host, as he was leaving him, "you, fellow, have starved me; a nice way indeed of treating the Gamana of a son-in-law. Oh dear, I am dying of hunger and thirst."

XX. GEWALA YAKSEYA, or *House demon*, lives in the dwellings of men. These demons are innumerable. They are the spirits of those, who lived and died in the houses they now haunt, and who on their deathbed had thought much more of the money or other valuables they had hoarded up in the house,† than of their souls.

* About an hour or so before a bridegroom accompanied by his friends arrives at the house of the bride, a person, named for the occasion *Gamana* or *messenger*, is sent forward with a number of betel leaves equal to the number of people, who accompany the bridegroom. The Gamana is to give these betel leaves to the bride's friends, together with the large *pingo* of plantains called *Gira-mul-tada*, which in the Maritime districts is always a *sine qua non* of the presents, which a Singhalese bridegroom carries to his bride's house.

† The Singhalese, especially the poorer classes, generally secrete their money in holes dug in the floor, or in the walls of their houses. In a case of burglary which was tried at Kandy before the Supreme Court about a year ago, it was

They are fond of throwing into confusion the cooking utensils and crockery, and of continually opening and shutting the boxes in the house, if the inmates do not take care to secrete the keys, unobserved by the spirits. The jingling of coin, the sound of strange footsteps, and the creaking of door-hinges are frequently heard. The demon does not like to see the inmates eat and drink and enjoy themselves. When these latter sit together at their meals, he gets so annoyed by the sight, that he seizes them by the hair and knocks their heads against each other. He is of course invisible to men, like all other demons, but is possessed of no power to inflict disease.* He belongs to the class called Mala Yakseyo.

XXI. Bodrima is a female demon, at first originating no doubt in the nursery, but at present believed to be a real existence. She is the ghost of a woman, who has died in child-birth. She is said to be heard at night, wailing and groaning in a peculiar manner; and if she sees a man passing by, she immediately springs on his back, and, fixing her fingers and long nails in his throat, tries to choke him to death. She however is afraid of women, and especially of a woman with a house-broom in her hand. When she is supposed to be heard at night groaning in her peculiar way, and approaching a house, the male portion of the inmates take care to remain inside, while the women, especially the elder, go out of the house with brooms, and abuse the demon with such a string of epithets and names, as would seem enough to drive, not only one Bodrima, but the whole race of demons from this terrestrial globe. On such occasions, people sometimes place at some distance from the house a lighted lamp and some betel leaves, which the demon is said to hold one by one over the lighted wick, and warm and foment her abdomen with. If she were to be fired at, there would

---

proved that a portion of the stolen property, consisting of some £3 or £4, had been concealed by the thief under the stone in the fire-place, as the least likely place to be suspected of concealing money.

* There are certain ceremonies performed to expel a Gewala Yakseya from a house, especially the *Perit* ceremony performed by Buddhist priests, generally during three days and four nights.

remain, it is said, nothing to be seen next morning, but a dead lizard. She is described as being so fat and short, that, when she moves, she appears rather to roll like a cask, than to walk.

XXII. The PRETAS are entirely a different race of beings from all that have yet been mentioned. They are the most helpless and miserable creatures in existence. They live only to suffer. Their life itself is a punishment, in which they expiate the sins of a previous state of existence. Their only aliment is spittle, or some other kind of loathsome matter, and even when they get a little of this, their destiny precludes them from making any use of it, and, like king Tantalus they can only look at it with a burning desire. The number of these beings is so great, that a Pali Buddhistical work, which lays down certain rules of discipline for the guidance of the followers of that religion, admonishes them not to throw stones or sticks, nor even to swing their arms when walking, lest they may strike a Pretaya and injure him. The Pretayo are invisible to men; they are of various degrees of stature, some reaching to the height of 3 or 4 hundred feet, others only of one or two feet. Their sufferings from hunger and thirst are indescribably dreadful, and to make their case the more miserable, their appetites are much stronger, than those of any other race of beings. They die several times in a day from sheer starvation, but owing to the inexorable destiny of their race are born again the same instant, to undergo the same round of sufferings over and over again, until they have completed the period of time allotted to them according to their respective sins, after which they are born in some other state of existence, either as Brahmas, dewiyo, men, inferior animals, or in hell, according to the merits of each, acquired in some other previous states of existence. Of course, they are the most loathsome looking creatures imaginable. Their skins hang about them in loose folds, and are so covered with dirt and vermin that they are supposed to emit a disagreeable smell, said to be perceived sometimes at a considerable distance. This smell is sometimes identified by a Singhalese with a peculiar unpleasant stench, often perceived near trees and bushes, caused as we believe, by the effluvia arising from decomposed leaves and sticks. Their bodies are literally mere skeletons, and as the fleshless ribs project on each side, they are obliged, when they wish to lie down, to lie on their backs.* Had Dante ever heard of Ceylon *Pretayo,* he would have been able to make his *Inferno,* terrific as it already is, still more terrific by the picture of a Pretaya figuring among those miserable beings, with whom he has peopled it. The Pretayo are not included in Demon worship. They are not possessed of power to injure a man in any other way, than by spoiling his appetite, which they effect by ***looking with desire*** at the food he is about to take; but this is a power, which is attributed to dogs and men and some other creatures, as well as to Pretayo. When any kind of food, especially meat, is sent from one house to another, care is generally taken to cover it well, and to put on the top of the cover a piece of iron of any kind or size, as a precaution both against the *Pretayo* and against the Yakseyo demons, who otherwise might affect it with the mysterious influence, which ***looking at*** it would produce. Children are seldom fed in the verandah of a house, and a Singhalese mother would rather die than allow her child to eat anything in the open compound or yard of the house. Even a medical decoction, during the process of being prepared on a fire, is not considered safe from this mysterious influence, and a piece of iron is often tied for protection to the vessel, which contains the preparation.

The Pretayo, like the ***Brahmas, Asuras, Cumbhas, Gandharwas, Garundhas,*** and ***Nagas,*** are creations of Buddhism, and not of mere popular fancy.

The chief of all Ceylon demons is WAHALA BANDARA DEWIYO, or as he is more commonly termed, ***Wahala dewiyo.*** His principal temple, called *Gala cap-pu dewale,* is at ***Alutnuwera,*** a village about 11 miles from Kandy on the road to Colombo. This temple

---

* When a person sleeps on his back, the posture is derisively named *Preta Seyiyawa,* or the *sleeping posture of a Pretaya*; lying on the face is called *Manduka Seyiyawa* or the *sleeping posture of a frog;* lying on the right side with the right hand placed under the head is considered the most becoming posture in sleeping, and is called *Singha Seyiyawa,* or the *lion's sleeping posture.*

is believed by all Demon-worshippers to have been built in a remarkable manner; and the circumstance is often mentioned, as one of the proofs of the authority, which the Dewatawa is supposed to exercise over his subjects the demons. It is said that the demon chief, a long time ago, wishing to have a new temple constructed and consecrated to him, in place of the old one in which his service had till then been performed, ordered some thousands of his subject demons to cut and smooth down a rock, which was some seven or eight hundred feet high, so as to fit it for the site of the intended building, they were however to use no other tools, than the common jungle canes called *Way Well,** with which they were to rub the rock, till by mere friction it should be reduced to the desired level. The demons engaged in the work were, no doubt, those, who having violated his laws were then undergoing the sentence of hard labour. They however succeeded in executing the work in the manner directed in the course of a single night, and hence the name *Gala-cap-pu dewale.* Pilgrims from every

---

* *Way Well* is a climbing plant, which grows to considerable dimensions in the jungles of Ceylon. It is covered with a coating of short but very sharp thorns. One species of it is used as a *file* by the people of the inland districts for rasping the hard kernel of the nut of the *Sal* tree, of which they make a sort of pudding. Being a *Rattan* of great strength, it is used for a variety of purposes, such as making baskets, *rattaning* chairs and couches, and even for making rude suspension bridges in the secluded parts of the island. The following is a description of one of these bridges by Sir J. E. Tennent.

"One which crossed the falls of the Maha Welli Ganga, in the Kotmalie range of hills, was constructed with the scientific precision of an Engineer's work. It was entirely composed of the plant called by the Natives "Way Well," its extremities were fastened to living trees, on the opposite sides of the ravine, through which a furious and otherwise impassable mountain torrent thundered and fell from rock to rock with a descent of nearly 100 feet. The flooring of this aerial bridge consisted of short splints of wood, laid transversely and bound in their places by thin strips of the Way Well itself. The whole structure vibrated and swayed with fearful ease, but the coolies traversed it though heavily laden; and the European, between whose estate and the high road it lay, rode over it daily without dismounting"—*Sir J. E. Tennent's History of Ceylon, Vol.* I. *part* I. *ch:* iii.

part of the Island repair to this temple during all seasons of the year, hoping to get relief from some demon influence, with which they suppose themselves to be afflicted, and which appears to them to be irremovable by any other means. This is especially the case with those persons, most frequently women, who are supposed to be possessed by a demon. Dancing, singing and shouting without cause, trembling and shaking of the limbs, or frequent and prolonged fainting fits are considered the most ordinary symptoms of possession by a demon. Some women, when under this imaginary influence, attempt to run away from their homes, often using foul language, and sometimes biting and tearing their hair and flesh. The fit does not generally last more than an hour at a time; sometimes one fit succeeds another at short intervals; sometimes it comes upon the woman only on Saturdays and Wednesdays, or once in three or four months; but always invariably during the performance of any demon ceremony. On these occasions temporary relief is obtained by the incantations of the Cattadiya; but when it appears that no incantations can effect a permanent cure, the only remaining remedy is to go to *Gala kep-pu Dewale*, where the following scene takes place. When the woman is within two or three miles of the temple, the demon influence is supposed to come on her, and she walks in a wild, hurried, desperate manner towards the temple. When in this mood no one can stop her; if any attempt it, she will tear herself to pieces rather than be stopped. She walks faster and faster, as she comes nearer and nearer to the holy place, until at last, on reaching it, she either creeps into a corner, and sits there, crying and trembling, or remains quite speechless and senseless, as if overpowered by extreme fear, until the Capua begins the exorcism. Sometimes she walks to the temple very quietly, without any apparent influence of the demon on her, and that influence seems to come upon her, only when the exorcism begins. The principal room of the temple is partitioned off by curtains into three divisions, the middle one of which is the sanctum sanctorum of the God, as the demon chief is generally called. The Capua stands outside the outermost curtain, with the woman opposite to him. After the offerings of money, betel leaves, and silver ornaments* have been devoutly and ceremoniously laid in a sort of small box opposite to the Capua, he tells the god as if he were actually sitting behind the curtain at the time in a loud and conversational tone, and not in the singing ornamental style of invocations made to other gods and demons, that the woman (*naming her*) has come all the way from the village (*naming it*) situated in the Corle or district (*naming it*) to this temple, for the purpose of complaining to his godship of a certain demon or demons, who have been afflicting her for the last five years (*specifying the time she has been under the influence*); that she has made certain offerings to the temple, and that she prays most humbly that his godship may be graciously pleased to exorcise the demon, and order him never to molest her again. In this way he makes a long speech, during which the woman continues trembling and shaking in the most violent manner, sometimes uttering loud shouts. Presently the Capua puts to her the question, "*Wilt thou, demon, quit this woman instantly, or shall I punish thee for thy impudence*"? To this she sometimes replies, still trembling and shaking as before, "*Yes, I will leave her for ever,*" but, more generally, she at first refuses; when this happens, the Capua grasps in his right hand a good stout cane, and beats her most mercilessly, repeating at the same time his question and threats. At last, after many blows have been inflicted, the woman replies "*Yes, I will leave her this instant*"; she then ceases to tremble and shake, and soon recovers her reason, if indeed she had ever lost it. So she and her friends return home, congratulating themselves on the happy result of their journey; a

* One of these ornaments is often a *Carandua*, or conical box resembling a *dagoba*, made of silver, and intended as a sort of shrine or receptacle for some holy relic. A silver arrowhead and an image, made of a beaten plate of silver of about two inches in height, intended to represent the person suffering from the Demon influence, are also sometimes added to the other offerings. The money offered to a god or demon is always called *Panduru*, which means *ransom money*.

result, which is invariably the same in the case of every pilgrim to the temple. We know 30 or 40 women who have made this pilgrimage, only two of whom have ever again shown any symptoms of the return of demon possession. It is said that some 30 or 40 years ago, especially during the time of the Kandyan Kings, four bundles of canes were left at the temple by the Capua every evening before he returned home; that during the night loud shouts and cries and wailing were heard proceeding from the temple, and that the next morning, instead of bundles of canes, there were only small bits of them found dispersed here and there in the premises, as if the canes had been broken in flogging disobedient demons.

CHAPTER III.

How Demons inflict Disease.

The demons enumerated in the preceding pages are those, who are supposed to inflict disease on men, and who therefore principally figure in the various Ceremonies of Demon worship. They are supposed to exercise their malignant power by virtue of the Wurrun permission, which they have obtained for that purpose from King Wessamonny, from the principal demon chiefs, or sometimes from some of the gods themselves. Originally when they were in a lawless state, they enjoyed themselves to their hearts' content, by seizing men wherever they could and eating them up alive, like so many oysters. But after a time these liberties were restrained to a certain extent, and they were allowed to eat human beings, only when the latter happened to come under the shade of the tree on which they lived, or within a certain distance of whatever place they had made their residence. Lastly, cannibalism was wholly prohibited, and, in place of it, permission was given them to inflict disease, and thereby receive offerings, with which they were required to be content.

Their usual hours of stirring abroad are called *Yama*. These are 1st, the morning twilight, when there is still some degree of darkness over the earth; 2nd, Mid-day, about 12 o'clock; 3rd, the evening twilight before it has grown very dark; and 4th, Midnight about 12 o'clock. During these Yamas, they stir abroad, as much in search of human victims as by way of recreation. A Singhalese never travels during these Yamas, if he can help it; but if not, he takes care not to go alone (unless it be the midday Yama), unless the country is very thickly inhabited, for solitary travellers are most exposed to the attacks of the demons. There are also certain circumstances in the condition or disposition of an individual, which make it easier for a demon to inflict disease on him; these are—1, when the man is asleep; 2, when he has his person perfumed with fragrant unguents and oils; 3, when he travels in a palanquin at night; 4, when a woman is in labour; 5, when the predominant feeling in the mind of a girl at the moment of her arriving at puberty is grief, love, or fear; 6, when a person takes his meals when his mind is not at ease; and a variety of other occasions.

The usual haunts of the demons are, 1st, large trees, especially *Bo*, *Nika*, *Ruk-attana*, *Ironwood*, *Cohomba*, *Banyan*, *Kong*, *Ehella*, *Yakberiya*, and *Belli trees;** 2nd, paths and roads; 3rd, the junction of two or more paths; 4th, ferries and fords; 5th, wells and other places where people come for water; 6th, places, where there are two rocks close to each other; 7th places, where there are two large trees standing near each other; 8th, the seashore; 9th, thick groves of trees and pleasure gardens; 10th, the outskirts of Dewales (temples of the gods;) 11th, graves and graveyards; 12th, tops of rocks and hills; 13th, places where the noise of quarrels and loud voices is continually heard; 14th, streams of water; 15th, battlefields; 16th, woods composed principally of *Belli* trees; 17th, places where washermen wash clothes; 18th, old deserted houses; 19th, large open plains or fields; and 20th, sometimes (not often) close behind the dwelling houses of men.

At these places the demon frightens people not by actually seizing them, but by other means quite as effectual. He sometimes throws sand or stones at them, often handful after handful, along a considerable part of their way; sometimes he appears as a dark featured man on the road or among the bushes near it; or he only shews himself like the passing shadow of a man, followed immediately by a shower of sand or a loud crashing noise among the bushes, as if a number of elephants were actively engaged in beating down the jungle; or he presents himself in the disguise of an old man, or of a young woman with a child in her arms, or merely like a man with a white cloth wrapped round his person from the

---

* It is on this account, that a Singhalese seldom allows any of these trees to grow very large, when they are situated near his house. He generally cuts them down, before they become fit for the residence of a demon ; nor on the other hand will he willingly cut down one which is already very old, fearing it might provoke the demon, who is supposed to be living on it, and bring down implacable vengeance on himself and his family.

top of the head down to the ancles. Sometimes the travellers find the road blocked up by a large tree lying prostrate across it with all its branches and leaves quite fresh, and if they try to go some other way, they find themselves similarly obstructed by trees and thick jungle, in places where there were none before; or they hear a loud hoo* shout, which however nobody else in the neighbourhood hears, but they; or a large black dog, or a monkey gives them chase; or they hear the sound of footsteps behind them, as of somebody coming up, but on turning round they see no one, and so they continue their journey, but hardly move a fathom before they hear the same sound again, more distinct and louder, and yet there is nobody to be seen; or when they are quietly moving on, they receive near a certain large tree a smart blow on the back from the cold open hand of somebody, who is no where to be seen; sometimes they see a man, a stranger, crossing their path at a short distance in front; or they see a man standing a little out of the road appearing at first to be of the ordinary stature of men, but gradually becoming taller and taller, till he overtops the neighbouring cocoanut tree itself. A Singhalese, to whom any of these things happens, is sure to be so much frightened, as to get some serious illness; on some, their superstitious terrors have had so strong an effect that they have dropped down on the spot perfectly senseless, and have been carried home in a hopeless state, and died within a few days; some have managed to run home but have been taken ill there, and have either died, or recovered only after three or four months of suffering, while others have become raving maniacs for the rest of their lives.

Although demons are said to shew themselves in these ways to men, yet the opinion of those, who may be called the more orthodox of the demon-worshippers, is that these apparitions are not the demons themselves, but certain puppet-like spectres, which

* A *Hoo* shout is one peculiar to the people of this island. It consists of a loud, single, guttural sound, uttered as loud as a man's lungs permit. A quarter of a mile is generally considered to be the distance at which a loud Hoo can be heard.

they create and present to the eyes of men, in order to frighten them; that the demons themselves are millions of miles distant from the earth; and that on these occasions of sending forth these spectres, and on every other occasion, whether during demon ceremonies, or at any other time when they are supposed to be present, they do not come themselves, but send their *dristia*, with or without the spectres, according to the circumstance of each case, or merely according to their own whim. By *dristia*, which means literally "sight," or "look," is meant that, although they are not personally present, yet they have the power of "looking" at what is going on below, and of doing and attending to every thing required of them, as if they were actually present. This opinion however is one, which is confined to the more learned of the demon worshippers; the more ignorant believe that the demons themselves are bodily present at these scenes, although they assume some sort of disguise, whenever they choose to make themselves visible to men.

When a man is frightened by a demon, and has the influence of that demon upon him, it is called TANICAMA, which literally means "*loneliness*" or "*being alone.*" Fright is in most cases a necessary agent in bringing down *Tanicama* on a man; but it is also possible that a person, who has neither been frightened by a demon, nor been ten yards from his own door for five or six months, may also get the Tanicama influence on him. In this case, the explanation is, that the demon has taken advantage of some unguarded moment in the daily life of the man, as when he has been sitting in the open compound of his house, or when he has happened to go to the back of his house at any of the Yamas, when a demon has happened to be in the vicinity; or when he has eaten roasted fish or eggs, while sitting outside in his Verandah on a Wednesday or Saturday. In this case the man is neither frightened by anything, nor even aware of his danger at the time.

When Tanicama comes upon a man, he falls sick and even when a man is ill from some other cause, no matter what, he very often gets the Tanicama, especially when the sickness is getting worse

The more dangerous and critical a disease is, the surer is Tanicama to come upon the sick man; and when the disease appears to be past all hopes of a cure, the *Tanicama* influence becomes strongest, and the demons remain in the very neighbourhood of the sick man's house, if not near his bed. The sound of footsteps, of the violent shaking of trees and bushes, sudden loud sounds, as of striking with whips and sticks, and similar other tokens of their presence and of their joy at the expected death, are supposed to be heard around the house. These ominous signs are called *Holman*. It is on this account, that so many demon ceremonies are performed, when a person is sick, from the commencement of the sickness to its termination.

The literal meaning of the word Tanicama gives us a key towards the understanding of many of the mysterious and wonderful circumstances connected with this part of our subject, especially when it is taken in connection with the other doctrine of Demonism already alluded to, viz., that, though a demon try his utmost by means of terrible apparitions or by actual seizure to frighten a man and give him the Tanicama, which results in sickness, yet the man will seldom get ill, if he do not get frightened.

Among many hundreds of instances of sickness, which we have heard of, as the consequences of Tanicama, the following is one, which came within our own knowledge a few years ago; and we give it here, merely to enable the reader to form some idea of the superstitious fears of a Singhalese, and of the strange pranks, which imagination plays with him.

One evening about 8 o'clock, some four years ago, we happened to take a walk to the seashore, which was not very far from our house. It was a bright moonlight night, and the sky was glowing with the brilliancy of thousands of stars. We were accompanied by two men, of whom one was a young man, whose name was Baba. The heat was unusually great, so we remained more than an hour on the seabeach on account of the cool sea breeze. The greater part of that hour was taken up by one of our two companions relating ghost stories, to which Baba, like every other Singhalese of his condition was an attentive listener. The road, by which we must return, was a narrow footpath flanked on both sides by thick bushes. Near this path, and about half way between the house and the seashore, was a large *bo* tree situated in an old graveyard, both of which had always had a bad name among the neighbours, as being haunted by demons, who, it was said, had on diverse occasions frightened many people even in broad daylight. In returning, we had of course to pass this tree and had hardly passed it ten paces, when Baba, giving one of those terrible fierce shrieks of despair and fear, which can hardly be described, threw his arms round the other man, trembling and panting in the most remarkable manner, and the next moment he dropped down senseless on the ground, perspiring most profusely. The other man, who was himself only a few degrees this side of the limits of a fainting fit, managed however to take up the terrified Baba and carry him home. Baba's father and mother having come, a Cattadiya was sent for; in the mean time one of the neighbours pronounced some incantations and the *pirit* charm over the sick man, who in a little while regained his senses. When the Cattadiya came, more charms were pronounced in an inaudible voice, at the conclusion of which some knots were made in the hair of the sick man's head, and some charmed cocoanut oil was rubbed on his forehead, temples, breast, nails, and on the crown of the head. He was then removed to his own house, accompanied by the Cattadiya and his friends.

When Baba was afterwards asked what had frightened him so much, he said that, as he was coming along behind us, he heard, near the large tree, a sort of growl, like that of a fierce dog muzzled, and on looking in the direction he saw a large head peering over a bush from behind the trunk of the large tree.

The morning after this occurrence, Baba was reported to be very ill. In the afternoon we saw him, and found him suffering from a raging delirious fever. Two days afterwards, the ceremony of *Sanni Yakum Neteema* or the *Dance of the Sanni demons* was performed, during which, about 3 or 4 o'clock in the morning, when the offerings were being dedicated to the demon *Sanni Yakseya*, the sick man exclaimed, pointing to one of the *Tatu* or altars, "*there, there, that is the person, whom I saw near the large tree the other day—there he is eating the rice;*"* the next minute he added, "*there now he is going away.*" Of course the eyes of all were turned in that direction, but there was nobody to be seen. The next day the man was better, and three days afterwards perfectly well.

Now in this case, it is plain, that either the man's own imagination, which must have been in a state of very great excitement, as he was passing the tree, conjured up to his sight the semblance of a demon, or that some one wishing to pass off a joke, had concealed himself behind the tree and shewed himself in the manner mentioned above. Of these two, the latter is not very probable, as few Singhalese have the courage to remain after sunset in a place supposed to be haunted; that the former is more probably the truth, is apparent from the fact, that the man recovered from his illness soon after the performance of that particular ceremony, which was believed by him, as well as by all demon-worshippers, to be an effectual remedy for diseases brought on by circumstances like those in his case. That the man's imagination was during all the time in a state of high and morbid excitement, is further proved by his pointing out, during the course of the subsequent ceremony, what he considered to be the demon that had appeared to him near the tree.

---

* The rice alluded to is that which is served out on the *Tatu* as an offering to the demons.

CHAPTER IV.

SPELLS OR CHARMS IN GENERAL.

In every demon ceremony, which is performed either to cure or inflict sickness, or to protect a person from becoming liable to any "demon sickness" at all, the effective agents, which influence the demons, and, through them, the disease, are CHARMS or spells, Invocations, and *Dolla* or offerings, especially the first with or without the two last. Like the sciences and the Literature of the Singhalese (with the exception of their Elu poetry), charms were originally introduced from the neighbouring continent. India, in those remote times, was to Ceylon and other neighbouring countries, what Greece was a little later to the rest of Europe. Wijeyo from India colonized it in the sixth century before Christ, and the literature and sciences of the Vedas naturally came with him, or soon after, until they were partly, but not wholly, superseded, two centuries afterwards by Buddhism and its literature. But Demonism had taken so strong a hold of the popular mind long before the time of Wijeyo, that nothing could displace it, and when any accessions were offered to it in subsequent times in the form of new charms and demons, it seems to have incorporated them with avidity into its old system.

Almost every charm begins with the words *Ohng Hreeng*, which, in Sanscrit, are an invocation to the Hindoo Trinity. The Cattadiyas of this country, who are not worshippers of that Trinity, not understanding the purport of the words, but attributing to them some mysterious magical properties, have, in a great many instances, prefixed those words to Singhalese charms, in which the virtues and omnipotence of Buddha are described in a very grandiloquent style, to the exclusion of those of the Hindoo triad. Sometimes however the names of Brahma, Vishnu, Siva and other Hindoo deities are found mixed with those of Buddha and other Buddhist divinities in irretrievable confusion in the same charm. Almost every charm, whether Singhalese, Sanscrit, or Tamil, ends with the word *Eswah*, which is a corruption of the Sanscrit term *Swaha*, corresponding in meaning to *Amen.**

The Charms or *Mantra*, as they are called, are generally in Sanscrit, Tamil, or Singhalese, but a few are written in other languages, such as Arabic, Persian, Telugu, Malayalim, Bengali, and others. Sometimes in one charm a mixture of many of these languages is used. Sometimes no language seems to have been used. In this last case, instead of any intelligible language, there seems to be a collection of barbarous sounds without meaning. Whether this is the *Paisachi*, which Colebrooke represents the Hindoo dramatists making their demons speak on the stage, we are not able to say.† It is however probable, that much of what now seems to be no better than gibberish may at one time have been an intelligible language, which, through its transmission from one illiterate Cattadiya to another, through being transcribed from one Ola into another by men not well acquainted even with their own language, and from the peculiar pronunciation used in the recitation of a charm, may have become so far distorted and changed from what it was, as to be reduced to its present condition. We fear we cannot give any correct idea of this peculiar pronunciation; it consists in a very rapid utterance, in which guttural and nasal sounds principally predominate, rendering for the moment even the plainest of Singhalese charms quite an unintelligible jargon; and to aggravate the evil still more, the recitation of a charm is *generally* performed in a low under tone of voice, scarcely audible to any one.‡

---

* *Swaha* is also a term, indicative of a certain *Fire-Offering* made to the god of fire, alluded to in Sanscrit works. The wife of the god of fire is called *Swahache Hoctabukpria*——*Amara Cosa.*

† Asiatic Researches Vol. VII. p. 199. quoted also by Turner, in his Introduction to the Mahawanso.

‡ One of the most remarkable facts, connected with Sorcery or Magic, is, that in all countries and ages of the world, where the Black Arts have ever been cultivated, the incantations to evil spirits have always been pronounced in a low muttering voice, as is still the practice both here, and in continental Asia and Africa.

The virtue and efficacy of a charm however consist, it is said, not so much in the meaning of the language used, as in a peculiar arrangement and combination of certain letters, each having its own peculiar power. According to this classification, some letters are called *poisonous*, others *deadly*, a third class *fiery*, a fourth *quarrelsome*, and a fifth *causing banishment.* On the other hand there are others called *prosperous*, some *pleasure-giving*, a third and a fourth class *health-giving* and *friendly*, and a fifth *divine;* while a few are called *neutral.* Then again, these letters, when arranged and combined in a certain order, have different virtues—virtues much stronger, than those of single letters. Each of these combinations of letters is sacred to a certain demon, for whom it has an unaccountable, mysterious, and irresistible fascination, from which he cannot free himself. The mysterious virtues of all these combined characters in a charm, are sufficient to overpower and enslave the most powerful demons to the will of the Cattadiya. To make a charm still more irresistible, flattery and entreaties are employed, or the terrible power of king Wessamonny is invoked, or the omnipotence of Buddha, and all set off in language the most horrible* to the ears of a demon-worshipper.

Native authors maintain that Brahma himself was the original author of charms, but that the science, as they call it, was afterwards amplified and improved by nine Irshis or learned pundits, who lived in India some thousands of years ago. It is divided into eight different parts called *Carma* or acts, according to the different character of the subjects it treats of. These are 1, *Mohana* or the power of inducing swoons; 2, *Stambana* or illicit sexual intercourse; 3, *Otchatana* or the expulsion of demons; 4, *Aakarsana* or compelling the attendance of demons; 5, *Wibeysana*

---

* The most prominent feature in the language of Singhalese charms is an endless repetition of such terms as *red blood, heart's blood, eat his lungs, graves, corpses, living corpses, suck his blood, tear open his heart, suck the marrow, a cloth dipped in blood, eat his heart, break his neck and suck the blood*, and many others, which have a very appalling effect on the timid, superstitious mind of a demon-worshipper.

or destruction by discord; 6, *Marana* or causing death; 7, *Tambanaya* or power of imprisoning; and 8, *Paysana* or power of curing diseases. To each of these acts are assigned certain seasons, days, and hours, in which alone anything relative to it can be performed with any hopes of success. Thus, Wibaysana must be performed during the eight hours elapsing between 6 P. M. and 2 A. M. at night, during the season called *Wasanta;* Otchatana, during the ten days intervening between the 10th and 20th day of the season called *Gunhana;* Marana, in the season *Wassana,* from the 20th day of the month, which commences that season, to the 10th day of the next month; Aakarsana, during the season *Sasat;* Stambana, from the 10th to the 20th day of the season *Haymanta;* Mohana, from the 20th day of the month, which commences the season *Sisira,* to the 10th of that which closes it; and Paysana and Tambana, during every part of the year.*

It is believed that there are, or at least there were, in this Island 240,000 different charms or spells of every kind, belonging to the art of Necromancy. An old legend says, that once upon a time, long before the landing of king Wijeyo upon these Coasts, one of the kings of this Island, wishing to marry from a royal family, proceeded to Ayodhia pura (Oude) and being introduced to the royal family of that country on the continent, was permitted to select for his queen one out of the seven daughters of the king. Upon this, being anxious to ascertain what their accomplishments were, he asked each of them, what she was most skilled in. One replied that she was skilled in the magical arts of sickening and killing people by means of *Hooniyan* charms; another replied, that she could bring immediate death on any one by means of *Pilli* charms; a third said that she could injure men

* Although there is not much difference of seasons in this Island, yet Singhalese writers have divided the year into six seasons. viz. 1. *Wasanta* which corresponds to April and May; 2, *Gimhana* (hot] which, corresponds to June and July; 3, *Wassana* [rainy] to August and September; 4 *Sarat* [dry] to October and November; 5, *Haymanta* [dewy] to December and January; and 6, *Sisira* [cool] to February and March.

by *Angam* charms; three others also replied in the same way, mentioning some particular department of Sorcery, in which they were most skilled, and by which they could bring diverse calamities on men; but the seventh and last princess said that she knew none of those in which her sisters were accomplished, but that she was well learned in the other class of charms, by which she could restore to health and life men suffering from the former. Upon this, the King of Ceylon, being highly pleased with her, selected her to be his Queen, and brought her away to his country. The other sisters being offended at this as an insult offered to them, determined to take their revenge. For this purpose they collected from all parts of the world every kind of charm, that was productive of evil to man, and inserting them in some peculiar manner in a pumpkin* sent it to their sister in Ceylon, as a present. Their object was to destroy their sister and her kingdom by its means, for on being touched by the hand of the person, for whom it was intended, it was to set on fire both that person and everything else within a hundred *Yoduns*.† But while the man, who carried it, was on the sea on his way to the Island, it set fire to his head, and then fell into the sea, from which it was afterwards picked up by a certain god, and presented to the King of Ceylon. These evil spells together with the charms in the healing department, which his own Queen knew, constitute the 240,000 alluded to above. Whatever particle of truth there may be in the story, it is certain that a majority of the charms now in use among the Singhalese were introduced in times much later, than those indicated by this legend.

---

* The pumpkin was selected for this purpose, because nothing else in the whole universe could hold such dangerous materials without being immediately burned to ashes! In the Ceremony of *Hooniyan Kerema*, by which all evil influences produced by any malignant charms are sought to be removed, a pumpkin is placed before the sick man, and after ordering, by means of incantations, all such evil influences to "descend to the pumpkin," the Cattadiya cuts the fruit in two, and then throws it into the sea or some other place of water.

† A *Yoduna* is 16 miles.

Though a charm be ever so good in the number and proper disposition of those peculiar combinations of letters we have already mentioned, and though it be complete in all other respects, yet it can have no power for any practical purpose, unless it be subjected to a certain process or ceremony called JEEWAMA, which literally means, "the endowing with life." This it is, that makes a charm efficacious for good or for evil. A Jeewama is considered to be a ceremony of greater or less difficulty and danger, according as the object of the charm is considered to be more or less easy of accomplishment. For instance, the Jeewama of a charm to cure a gripe or a headache is attended with no danger, whilst that of another, intended to cause the death of a person or to seduce the affections of a girl, is supposed to be fraught with great danger to the life of him, who performs the ceremony. This danger arises from demons, who endeavour to prevent in various ways the accomplishment of the man's object. For, should the charm be perfected by the uninterrupted progress of the Jeewama, the demon would be bound, nolens volens, to accomplish the object aimed at by the charm. Hence their anxiety to interrupt a Jeewama, and to frighten away those engaged in it; the consequences of that fright to the men, being sickness and death.

When a Cattadiya is asked why it is that he cannot now do any of those wonderful things, which his predecessors of earlier days are said to have done, and which his omnipotent charms profess to be able at any time to effect, his answer is invariably an argument founded on this danger and difficulty of the Jeewama ceremony.

Every charm has a sort of rubric appended to it, in which the object of the charm* is stated, and instructions are given in what

* Some people have been so anxious to prevent others from making use of any of those "tried" [Singhalese *Atdutu*] charms, in whose efficacy they have the firmest belief, that they have managed to render their own manuscript copies mere sealed books to the rest of the world, by writing the rubric in a way unintelligible to those not initiated into the mystery. For this purpose, they

place and manner the Jeewama is to be performed, together with a list of the offerings required on the occasion.

The Jeewama of some charms is as follows.—The Cattadiya, or whoever has undertaken the task,* repairs to a grave at one of the Yamas, and prepares what is called a ***Mal Bulat tatuwa*** or ***table of flowers and betel leaves;*** this is a chair or something similar, with a piece of white † cloth or a green plantain leaf spread on it; on this cloth or leaf must be placed nine different kinds of flowers, a few of each kind, the yellow flowers of the Areca and the red flowers of a small shrub called ***Rat Mal*** being generally of the number. With these is mixed some sandal wood powdered fine and mixed with water; sometimes a few betel leaves,‡ with a copper coin, are added. The whole of this is called ***Mal Bulat tatuwa.*** On this table is placed a thread or thin string called ***Kan-ya Nool*** or ***Virgin Thread,*** so called from its having been spun by a virgin from native cotton.‖ This thread is coloured

---

generally use a language like that, which Reynolds describes in his *Pickwick Abroad* and *Mysteries of London* as used by the abandoned desperados of London.

* Excepting in regular ceremonies, which are performed to cure a disease, persons other than professional Cattadiyas often engage in minor matters of the Art, such for instance as the "trying" of a single charm, unless its Jeewama be considered to be one attended with danger.

† *White* has been the emblem of purity among all nations and in all ages of the world.

‡ These betel leaves must be taken from a plant, from which none have been previously removed by men for the purpose of chewing.

‖ *Kan-ya Nōol* threads are used in almost every Demon ceremony, but, what particular virtue they have, or what mysterious relation they bear to demons, I have never been able to ascertain. There are certain rules which are to be observed by the girl in the spinning of this thread; but they are never strictly observed now a days, lest a strict adherence to them may make her liable to Tanicama or some other similar calamity. By these rules the girl must first wash herself, and then putting around her neck a necklace of *Rat mal* flowers, with her hair thrown loose on her shoulders, she must sit on the threshold of the door of her house, looking towards the setting sun about 6 P. M., and then spin the mysterious thread.

yellow by rubbing it with a piece of saffron.* Another table called *Pidayni tatuwa* or *Offering altar* is then made, with the green sticks of a shrub called *Gurulla* or *Burulla* for its legs, and is covered with the inner white bark of the plantain tree, and the broad green leaves of the *Haburu* plant.† On this altar are placed *Etta Etty* or *Seeds*, being five different kinds of seeds roasted well on a fire, the *Hat Malu*, or *Seven Curries*, consisting of vegetables, fish, and flesh of land animals, and a little boiled rice.‡ A fire

---

* *Saffron* is an article used both in the rites of Demonism and in those of Capuism. In the latter, the offerings, which consist principally of money and images of silver, must be rubbed over with saffron, and then wrapped up in a piece of a saffron leaf, before they are placed on the altar. A quantity of water held in a species of jug called *Cotalay* is also coloured and perfumed with saffron; this water is thrown by the Capua on the persons of the devotees as Holy Water.

† *Haburu* is a sort of potatoe, cultivated in the dwelling gardens of most of the poorer classes of the Singhalese. It also sometimes grows wild. It has no stem nor branches. The leaves are heart-shaped and very large, sometimes measuring 5 feet by 4. The root is large, being sometimes about a foot in diameter, and three or four in length, perfectly cylindrical and of uniform thickness from one end to the other; if the plant be allowed to grow long, this root becomes a sort of stem rising to a height of four or five feet from the ground, with a crown of five or six leaves on its summit. This stem (when there is one), and the root are used by the people for food. It produces a sharp, biting sensation, when taken into the mouth, so much so indeed, that it is with great difficulty that it is swallowed. Some kinds however, which have been carefully cultivated, do not possess this unpleasant quality in any great degree, and some are almost entirely free from it. It is recommended by native doctors as a very valuable medicine to those subject to piles. There are several species of Haburu, most of which are used as food. One or two kinds are especially prized for making Curries. *Cohila Cola* is one of the most favourite dishes of a Singhalese, and it belongs to this genus. Its medicinal properties too are considered to be very great. A medicine called *Cohila Patmay* is prepared from it for those suffering from piles, and we have reason to believe in its efficacy.

‡ For fish, a piece of dry fish, and for flesh, a piece of skin from an old leather sandal are generally substituted for the sake of convenience. The rice directed to be used on this occasion is the kind called *El Sal* or Hill Rice,

is then made on the grave, with *Pas Pengiri dara* or the wood of five different kinds of trees, the fruit of which is sour to the taste, such as orange trees, lime trees, citron trees, and others of that kind. On this fire is placed an earthen pot containing an egg, and a gentle fire is kept up, till the egg is completely boiled. While this boiling is going on, the Cattadiya lies down on the grave at full length on his back, and pronounces his charm in a low tone a certain number of times, 3, 7, 9, 16, 48, 49, 108, 128, or 133 times, and in some cases so many as 1000 times, each time taking care to throw a small quantity of powdered resin into a pot containing some hot live cinders.* The resin produces a strong-scented thick smoke, with which the Malbulat Tatuwa and the Pidayni Tatuwa are performed. This is done generally as many times as the charm is recited. He then sits up on the grave, and taking into his hand a cock pronounces over it another charm. Next he takes the Kan-ya Nool thread, and, pronouncing a charm over it, makes a knot in it. The charm is recited several times over the thread, and each time a knot is made in it, the firepot being kept smoking, with resin under the thread. Sometimes all this has to be repeated at two succeeding Yamas, after which the charm is considered to be complete. The whole of this ceremony is called *Jeewama.* The charmed thread is brought away, and used for the purpose, and in the way, directed: for instance, if the object be to cure sickness, the thread is tied round the arm, or the neck, or the waist of the sick person; if the charmed substance be not a thread, but something else, as a betel leaf, and if the object of the charm be to gain the affections of a woman, the betel leaf is given to her through some proper agent.

The above is only a general description of a Jeewama ceremony. For each charm has its own particular Jeewama, differing from all

---

which is considered to be the best; yet in point of practice rice of any kind is used.

* The firepot or the Chafing dish is mentioned by Lane in his *Modern Egyptians*, and seems to be as much in demand among the sorcerers of Egypt, as among the Cattadiyas of Ceylon.

others both in the offerings it requires, and in the time, place, and manner of its performance. However the Kan-ya Nool, altars, flowers, and the smoking firepot, are always required; and graves, generally.

An ordinary *Aaraksa Nool*, that is a charmed thread worn about the person as an amulet against Tanicama, requires no greater Jeewama ceremony than this—the Cattadiya having gone to the back of the house with a Kan-ya Nool, some live cinders in a cocoanut shell or a tile, and a little saffron and resin, pronounces his charm in the usual low muttering tone, all the while perfuming the thread with the resin smoke, and making a few knots in it, equal sometimes to the number of times he pronounces the charm. All this does not take up more than 30 or 40 minutes. But in certain other Jeewamas, such as those relating to many kinds of *Hooniyan* and *Pilli*, whose object is the destruction of some person, these things are done on a greater scale, and are said to be attended with great danger to the lives of those engaged in them.

The danger, it is said, consists in this,—When the Cattadiya is going on with his incantation, but particularly about its conclusion when the virtues of the charm are becoming perfected, demons begin to arrive on the spot, one after another, generally in the disguise of beasts and serpents, such as monkeys, black dogs, elephants, tigers, Cobra-de-Capellos, polongas, and sometimes in the shape of old wrinkled grey headed men and women, with the exception of the last demon who appears like a man. Each of these, as he arrives, must be presented with the particular offering appointed for him, such as an egg, a fowl, some boiled rice, a young king-cocoanut, a few drops of blood, or something else as directed in the charm itself; any mistake or delay in presenting the offering being followed by immediate death or incurable sickness to those engaged in the ceremony. The demons, when they approach the scene, do all they can to frighten away the men, either by felling large trees near the spot, or by surrounding the men with a ring of burning jungle, or by creating a thick darkness, such as Milton speaks of in his *Paradise Lost*, or by uttering loud screams and howls like the roaring of thunder. All this the demons are said to do, in order to prevent the success of the charm: for if the virtues of the charm were to be perfected by the Jeewama, the demons would be spell-bound to act like slaves in effecting that, which the charm is intended for. Hence their anxiety and efforts to frustrate its success. These efforts, it is said, have generally been successful, and many a story is related of men found lying dead on the scene of a Jeewama, and of others, who lived raving maniacs for the rest of their lives, or who died a few days after their attempt to perform the ceremonies, from a delirious fever which no medicine or demon ceremony could cure.

Charms, it is said, do not retain their virtues beyond a certain period; some retaining them only 50 years, while others retain them 100, 300, 700, 900, 1000, 1900, 2700, or 3300 years. Those few alone, of which Brahma himself was the author, retain their efficacy for ever. Besides, the loss of a single letter which belongs to a charm, or the addition of one which does not, or any other alteration, though the smallest possible, is supposed to affect it equally; in this latter case, however, there is said to be a certain method of revising the charm and of restoring its original reading by means of a certain magic table called *Siddhi Chakkray.*

The principal works on the subject of charms are *Narayena, Mayrutantria, Mantra chinta Mania,* and *Mantra Kakse,* which are all in Sanscrit. Less important works treating both of Demon ceremonies and of charms in general, are *Mantra Mala Tecka, Sanka pala Widia, Cola Widia, Bahirawa Widia, Bahirawa Calpe, Cuhara Widia, Sagal Asna, Cumara Widia,* and *Asura Widia,* which are partly in Singhalese and partly in Sanscrit. There are many Cattadiyas now living, who have more or less studied these works, and are celebrated among their countrymen for their professional attainments, among others *Caduru Pokuna,* and *Dandawe Ganitaya* and *Ratuwatte Cattadiya* in the district of Suffragam.

We have translated a few charms for the amusement of the reader; and in doing so, we have selected those, which would be most intelligible. The following is one which is intended to drive a man mad—

"Oh Brahma, Vishnu and Siva! I make my adoration to you! Oh, come thou, Hanumana! Oh, come, thou god, Hamunanta! Oh, come thou, Madana! Oh, come, thou goddess, Madana! Come thou, Baddracali! Come, thou goddess, Baddracali! Come thou, Curumbara! Come, thou god, Curumbara! Oh, come thou, Maha Sohona! Oh, come, thou god, Maha Sohona! Come thou, Gopolla! Come, thou god, Gopolla! Come thou, Reeri! Come, thou god, Reeri Yakseya! Oh Samayan, come! Oh, come, thou god of Samayan! Come thou, Wata Cumara! Come, thou god, Wata Cumara! Oh, come thou, Calu Yakseya! Come, thou god, Calu Yakseya! Oh Vishnu, come thou! Oh Vishnu's Avatar, come! Come thou, Ayiyanayaka! Come, thou god, Ayiya-nayka! Come from on high! Come from below! Come from all directions! Come from all parts of the universe! Come, all the dewo and all the dewatawas! * Come, all ye demons! Come, all ye demon chiefs! Come, thundering from the sky! Come, making the earth tremble as ye come! Ye demons Encadawara and Malcadawara, all ye dewo and dewatawas, ye male demons and female demons, look at this human being from head to toe! Look at his bones, his sinews, his joints, his neck, his blood, his lungs, his heart and his intestines of 32 cubits in length. Look, look at them! And Oh! receive this human being, as a sacrifice unto you! Take him for yourself! Take him! I dedicate him to you. I dedicate him to you. I dedicate him to you with his dummala † incense. Look at him and accept him. Let this be so."

---

* *Dewo* are the gods; *Dewatawas* are the inferior classes of gods and the superior classes of demons. But the Cattadiyas often carelessly apply the latter term to inferior demons too. In charms however, flattery being one of the means of drawing the attention of a demon, no distinction is observed in the application of these terms, as is obvious from the above charm.

† The incense offered to demons by the Sorcerers of this country is not frankincense and myrrh, as elsewhere in the East, but a species of very inflammable resin called *dummala*, which is obtained from the ground a few feet

Then come the directions for performing the Jeewama, which are as follow—"Make a Mal Bulat Tatuwa and three Pidayni Tatuwas on a grave. Use the Etta Etty, the Seven Curries, blood, boiled rice, opium, three lizard eggs, a cock, seven clusters of Rat Mal flowers, the ashes of burnt hair, and roasted meat for these altars. Make an image of wax, and write on it the name of the person, who is to be injured. Take then seven Kan-ya Nool threads, and pronouncing the charm 108 times, make seven knots in the threads, one in each. Put the image on an Areca flower, the first, which that tree has ever produced, and tie them up together by means of the threads. Then take this away and conceal it in the back roof of the house. The man will be insane from that day. To cure him, remove the image from the roof and throw it into a stream, and the man will recover his reason."

The following is a charm for curing any disease supposed to be caused by the demon Reeri Yakseya:—

"Brahma, Vishnu, and Siva! Adoration be to you! The demon Reeri Yakseya, who resides on the rock Mala Dola Gigiriana in the land of Sayurasla, came into this world from the womb of his mother Laytali by tearing himself through her heart, on Saturday in the month of Nawan, [corresponding to a part of February and part of March.] This demon wears a crown of fire on his head, a cloth of blood below his waist, and another cloth of blood above, thrown across his shoulders. He has the face of a

---

below the surface, and also from certain trees, which produce gums equally inflammable and also called dummala, of which the *Sal* tree is the principal.

The Ola books of the Singhalese being written with an iron stile, the characters are illegible, but by rubbing on them an oil extracted from dummala, mixed with the ashes of burnt rags, a black colour is imparted to the lines, and so the letters become very legible.

The practice of offering incense to beings considered to be superior to men, whether they are called gods or demons, is one which appears to have prevailed from the earliest times, and its origin would indeed be a very interesting subject of inquiry both in connection with the history of Ceylon Demonism, and in relation to the Jews, with whom it was usual to make an incense offering to Jehovah.

monkey; his feet are of a bloodred colour, and the rest of his person of a golden hue. He brandishes in one hand the Bludgeon, and in the other the Trap of death, by whose apparition he is attended. When he received his wurrun from Iswara, Sekkra, and Brahma, he repaired to a place where three roads met, and standing there, and licking at the same time two pieces of human bones, which he carried in his mouth, his whole person dripping with blood, he clapped his hands and bawled out so dreadful a cry of triumph and defiance, that even the gods of ten thousand worlds were struck with terror and dismay. When the four guardian gods of the world asked, if there was not any one in the universe powerful enough to subdue the demon, they were told that neither Iswara,* nor Brahma, nor Natha, nor Gandharwas, nor Garundas, nor Saman, nor any Sorcerer could do it. Upon this, the great, the glorious, the wonderful Vishnu took a jungle creeper, which grew on the Rock of Blood in Sayurasla Desey, which is situated beyond seven seas and pronounced over it this charm—Oh Brahma, Oh Siva, Oh Vishnu, Oh Walia, come! Come thou, Hanumanta! Come, all ye gods! Come, all ye demons! Come instantly! I bind, I bind. I confine, I confine. Be bound, be bound. Be confined, be confined. Let this be so. By pronouncing these words he bound and subdued the demon Reeri Yakseya. Therefore by the power of Vishnu, and the overthrow he gave thee that day, I compel thee, oh demon Reeri Yakseya, to be bound by my charm. I bind thee. Be thou bound, bound, bound.† I order thee to heal at once this disease, which thou hast brought on this human being. Let this be so.

"This charm is to be pronounced over a thread‡ or some oil,‖ afterwards the oil must be rubbed over the person, or the thread must be tied round his arm; and the patient will recover from that instant."

---

* *Iswara*, I believe, is another name of Siva.

† This repetition of the same word is characteristic of most charms, especially in that part in which its virtues are supposed to be concentrated.

‡ Whenever *threads* are mentioned in charms or in any thing else relating to Demonism, Kan-ya Nool threads are meant.

‖ When *oil* simply is mentioned, it is to be understood of cocoanut oil. But

The following is a charm for curing headache. It is to be pronounced over a little oil, which must be stirred incessantly with a piece of iron all the time that the charm is being pronounced.

"Oh Brahma, Vishnu, and Siva! I make my adoration to you! When Ginires dewatawi (she demon of fire), who resides in Ginires Coville (temple of fire), in the country of Ginires Daysa (land of fire), complained to Mangra Dewiyo of the fire which was burning in her head, he (Mangra Dewiyo) sent for milk from the breasts of the Seven Mothers of milk,* and with it put out the fire which was burning in her head; for which he had received Wurrun from sixty-four different persons. By the power he exercised that day, I do this day command that the headache, which troubles this person, do quit him instantly—do flee, flee this moment."

Although by far the largest majority of charms are either for inflicting or for curing diseases, yet there are many others for various other purposes, and in fact there can hardly be a wish of any kind, be it good or bad, which may not be gratified by charms. Among others, the following is one for inducing demons to throw stones into dwelling houses, so incessantly and so long, as to compel the inmates to desert the house.

"Oh Brahma, Vishnu, and Siva! Adoration be to you! The she-demon Calu Cambanee, who influenced the bile, the she-demon Narasingha, who influenced the wind, and the she-demon Sen

---

in some cases when it is expressly mentioned, a composition of several kinds of oil, called *Pas Tel* or the Five oils, is used. These five oils generally are Cocoanut oil, Gingelli oil, *Cohomba* oil, *Mee* oil, and Castor oil.

* There is a certain Dana or Almsgiving ceremony called *Kiri Ammawarunnay Dana* or the Alms of the Mothers of Milk, generally observed three months after the birth of a child. Besides other people, who are invited to the house to partake of food or Dana on the occasion, seven women, sometimes seven unmarried girls, named for the time *Kiri ammala* or Mothers of Milk, are made to sit apart from the others, and are treated to a breakfast of boiled rice, plantains, and a sort of jelly called "Milk," made of rice flour, jaggery or country sugar, and the juice of the cocoanut. The dishes of the others, who are treated on the same occasion, are different from these.

Cumari, who influenced the phlegm, in the disease, which afflicted the four great demons, who were the offspring of the great king Carma; the demon Sanni Yakseya, who influenced all the three, the Bile, the Wind, and the Phlegm; the demons, who produce disease by means of the Evil Eye and the Evil Mouth; and the demons and she-demons Takaree, Makaree, Kalaraksee, Yamadootee, Ailakkandi, Mailakkandi, Nanaroopee, Telokadewi, and Oddy Curumbara, these demons and she-demons, who afflict man with 98 diseases, and 99 infirmities, and subject him to the risks of 203 dangers, all you male and female demons, I bind you first by the power of the god Loka Natha; secondly, I bind you by the power of the glorious god Vishnu; thirdly, I bind you by the power of the worldfamous goddess Pattini; fourthly, I bind you by the power of the god Saman; fifthly, I bind you by the power of the god Dewol; sixthly, I bind you by the power of the god Canda Cumara; seventhly, I bind you by the power of Andungini Dewatawa; eighthly, I bind you by the power of King Wissamonny himself; ninthly, I bind you by the power of the Graha gods (the Planet gods); tenthly, I bind you by the power of the eight Guardian gods, who are in charge of the eight points of the sky. I bind you all. I bind you all by the power of all these gods. I do this by the same power which the great Prades Rusia* used. Do, as I do. Stay, where I tell you to stay. Go, where I tell you to go. Eat, burn, destroy, when I command you to eat, burn, and destroy. Let this be so."

The Jeewama of the above—"Put a Champica flower, a flower of the iron wood tree, and a stone on a Mal Bulat Tatuwa, placed on a grave, or at the point of junction of three roads, or near a tree, whose bark has a great deal of sap in it. Then place around the Mal Bulat Tatuwa a little blood, a little milk, a few flowers, and some *porri*,† each kind in a separate leaf. Then put up lights all round; having done this take some resin, and pronounce over it the

---

* Prades Rusia was the first man, who followed the profession of a Cattadiya.

† *Paddy*, as rice in the husk is called here, being put into a vessel and heated over a fire, splits open into large white flakes, which are called *porri*.

charm (not the above but the one used for consecrating resin), and hold up the smoking fire-pot to the Mal Bulat Tatuwa. Next, pronounce the above charm 108 times. Do this at three several Yamas. Lastly, take away the stone, and bury it in the ground under the stile of the garden fence, or at the back of the house. Then throw a stone at the house; and from that day, that house will be pelted with stones. To put a stop to the pelting remove the buried stone, and throw it into a stream or some other place of water, and the stone-pelting will cease from that day."

Charms may be divided into two great classes, viz., 1st—Those intended to inflict death, disease, or some other inconvenience upon men; 2nd—Those intended to counteract the first, and remove their evil consequences. Under the head of the first class come several departments of charms, chiefly HOONIYAN, ANGAM, and PILLI charms; under the second, BANDANA, DEHENA and a few others. These will be treated of in the succeeding chapter.

CHAPTER V.

Hooniyan Charms.

Codiwina or Hooniyan is the name given to evils of whatever kind inflicted by the agency of charms. Hence the charms which cause these have been denominated Hooniyan charms. There are said to be 84000 of these, of every degree of malignity, most of which more or less contribute to bring to an untimely death the man affected by their influence, though that event may be deferred for many years. Some Hooniyan charms have the effect of filling a house or garden with so many demons, that the owner finds it difficult to pass even a single night in the house, but if he take heart to do so, it is most probable that he and his family will fall sick, one after another, as if attacked by some contagious disease: others frighten him by hideous night dreams, or by sudden apparitions, even in broad daylight, of large black dogs trying to bite him, or of ugly monkeys grinning at him,* but who vanish the next moment from his sight.

Whatever may be the nature of the disease brought on a man by Hooniyan charms, that disease always resists every attempt to cure it by medicine, and invariably results in the death of the man, unless other remedies be applied in time, viz., those which charms alone afford. For although there are gods and god-worship (*ca-puism*), and Buddhistical *Pirit* and *Pirit Nool*,† that hold out to their votaries every protection against demons, and although these gods are beings immeasurably superior to the demons in power,

---

* These superstitions about demons assuming the disguise of monkeys to frighten men seems to have been current in the time of Shakespeare.

Caliban—" His spirits hear me..

" Sometimes like apes, that mow and chatter at me—

Tempest Act II. Scene II.

† *Pirit* is a certain Buddhist ceremony performed for the purpose of removing all sorts of demon influence; and *Pirit Nool* is a thread consecrated by that ceremony, and used as an amulet for the same purpose.

yet if a demon bring his malign influence to bear upon a man through the agency of Hooniyan charms, no power on earth below or in the sky above can save him, unless he resort to the very art, which in the hands of his enemies has injured him so much. Generally, if a man often gets sick, especially from rheumatic attacks, and if he frequently feels thirst accompanied by an unusual degree of heat in the blood, especially about the region of the chest, he will attribute it to Hooniyan charms and more so, if he recollects that he has an enemy in one of his neighbours: and even though he has no enemy, yet if his sickness seems to resist the skill of his physician, and if a burning sensation in his body is one effect of his sickness, and if he is often troubled by dreams in which black dogs, monkeys, and horrible looking men try to frighten him, he is sure that his sickness is a Hooniyan. If a man in climbing a tree, or in moving from the top of one tree to that of another on the ropes which connect them together (as is the case with cocoanut trees during the season of distilling Arrack), makes a false step and is thereby precipitated to the ground whereby he dies, the probability is that the calamity will be attributed to a Hooniyan*: and this probability will not be the less strong, because the man may sometimes happen to escape with only a few bruises and fractures; but it will, on the contrary, be much more strengthened by what the man himself relates, which generally amounts to this—that, while he was on the tree, he was thrown down by somebody whom however he did not see, or that he was frightened by some monstrous-looking being, which appeared and disappeared with the rapidity of lightning, or that he suddenly and most unaccountably felt giddy and faint and so lost his footing and fell; all which to the

* About twelve months ago, there was a lawsuit between one of our friends and another man, so they were not on the very best of terms with each other. Before the case was decided, the other man happened to fall from a cocoanut tree and died instantly. It was therefore imputed to a Hooniyan charm practised by our friend. And the two families are now at deadly enmity with each other.

minds of his friends are so many proofs of a Hooniyan cause, although some unfriendly wag of a neighbour might insinuate that the man was tipsy with Toddy rather than affected by a Hooniyan cause at the time. Suppose a man and his wife constantly quarrel and do not like each other's company, especially at the commencement of their matrimonial life, and neither of them can assign any adequate reason for it, then, although the man's friends will say that the woman is wholly to be blamed, and the woman's friends that the man is solely to be blamed, it is most probable however that both these sets of friends in their cooler moments will say that a Hooniyan must be the sole cause of this domestic misery. A young woman is betrothed to a young man, but sometime afterwards the match is broken off through the non-consent, say, of some of the girl's relatives, and she is therefore given in marriage to another young man, and in due course of time she gives birth to a child; if, during the pains of delivery, she suffers much, and is not easily delivered of her burthen, you will then hear but one word whispered in low accents from mouth to mouth among all the relatives and friends assembled there; and that word is Hooniyan. You may see some of these relatives standing in groups of 2 or 3 in the compound or behind the house, engaged in an earnest, anxious, grave, and whispering conversation, others hurrying here and there either in search of a skilful Cattadiya, or in making preparations for performing some special demon ceremony, although similar ceremonies had been performed months before in anticipation of such a calamity, a suspicion of which necessarily arose from the circumstances attending the marriage. Or you may see one Cattadiya, standing near the house, muttering his charms over a small tea-cup containing some cocoanut oil or over a thread; and another standing before the distressed woman, and with an "Arecanut Cutter"* cutting three limes,† at the

* An Arecanut Cutter is an instrument, which is found in every Singhalese house. As its name implies, it is used for cutting Arecanuts preparatory to their being chewed with betel leaves, chunam, and tobacco.

† The cutting of limes on this, and on every other occasion when it is intend-

same time pronouncing some short charms in a voice a little more audible than usual. And after all, if the woman dies, it only confirms the truth of what they had but surmised at first.

In most Hooniyan charms, a small image made of wax or wood, or a figure drawn upon a leaf or something else, supposed to represent the person intended to be injured, is necessary. A few hairs of his head, some chippings of his finger nails, and a thread or two from a cloth worn by him, and sometimes a handful of sand from a place on which he has left his footprint, are also required, when the image is submitted to the Jeewama, especially in Hooniyans directed against parties intending to marry. Also *Pas Lo* or *five metals*, that is nails made of a composition of five different kinds of metals, generally gold, silver, copper, tin, and lead, are driven into the image at all those points, which represent the joints, the heart, the head, and other important parts of the body. The name of the intended victim is also marked on the image. After the Jeewama, this image is buried in the ground in some suitable place, such as under the stile of the garden fence, or in some other spot, where the intended victim is likely to "*pass over*"* it. This "passing over" is essential to the success of a large majority of Hooniyan charms. After this, the image is either left in the same place, or is taken out and secreted in some other place according to the directions in the charm itself. In the case of some Hooniyans, which however form but a small minority, this "passing over" is not needed at all, as, for instance, in those intended to produce *impotency* in a man.

To ensure greater certainty of success to a Hooniyan charm, other precautions are also sometimes taken, such as ascertaining from the horoscope of the party the particular season or day or

---

ed as a part of a demon ceremony, is done in a particular manner; the lime is placed between the two blades of the Arecanut Cutter, where it is held firmly by slightly pressing with the fingers the two ends or handle of the "Cutter," while the charm is being pronounced over it. Then, as the last word or syllable of the charm is being pronounced, and before its sound can have time to die away, the fruit is at once cut in two by a single effort.

* *Panna-wana-wa* is the Singhalese term for this.

hour, in which some planet or planets appear to threaten him with some calamity, and regulating the time of performing the Hooniyan accordingly.

Hooniyan charms are considered to be so powerful, that, even if a person other than the one for whom the charm was intended happen to be the first to "pass over" the buried image, he too is injured in some degree; the diseases produced in such a case being generally sores, boils, and itches on the feet, especially on the soles. A man, who sees a boil on the sole of his foot, and knows that he has not been treading on any jungle thorns, immediately suspects that he must have been "passing over" a buried Hooniyan charm, intended either for himself, or for somebody else; and so the Cattadiya and his *Hooniyan kapeema* ceremony are soon put in requisition, together with the assistance of the physician, the Capua, the Astrologer, the Balicaraya, the Buddhist priest and the Soothsayer; who, each in his own way, contribute to the desired result; for the creed of a Singhalese is, not to wait for a cure from one source alone, but to avail himself of all within his reach, although the art of Sorcery is positive in its dogma, that an evil caused by that art can be remedied by it alone, and by none other.

The following are the names of a few Hooniyan charms, considered to be unfailing in their effects, together with a brief description of the nature of these effects.

1. *Marulu Pennuma.*—Causes madness—burning heat every where in the body—frequent deprivation of the senses—running into words and streams—shouting, weeping, using violent and abusive language—paroxysms of rage—fainting fits—eventual death.
2. *Dala Reeri Watey.*—Causes the demon to be always in the company of the man, which is a source of perpetual disease of every kind which at last results in death.
3. *Reeri Cuppey.*—Sickness till death—the demon's influence never leaves the man till after death.
4. *Maha Sohon Gini Maruluwa.*—Lays desolate whole villages, depopulating them by sickness or death.

5. *Mayga Patala Oddi Deheney.*—The man vomits blood—falls down senseless—in a short time dies.
6. *Bamba Dristia.*—The demon Reeri Yakseya shews himself to the man in the disguise of Brahma, several times in a day, which leads to sickness and death.
7. *Calu Cumara Murtuwa.*—Swoons and fits of insanity—discharge of blood in the case of females—dancing and uttering *hoo* cries—sudden death.
8. *Sanni Calu Cumara Murtuwa.*—Madness.
9. *Reeri Yak Murtuwa.*—During the wedding procession the bride will become mad, and the demon Reeri Yakseya will at the same time strike the bridegroom's head with his knuckles.
10. *Wada Yak Murtuwa.*—The wife gets mad—demons take possession of the house—sickness and death.
11. *Madena Cumara Murtuwa.*—Madness.
12. *Sanni Daepaney.*—Continual disturbance, noise, and apparitions of demons within the precincts of the family residence—the house becomes uninhabitable, shrieks, screams, and horrible cries are heard frequently at night.
13. *Sohon Gini Bandenay.*—Insanity and delirious fever—rheumatic attacks—pains in all the joints—paralysis—death at the end of three months, if not cured sooner. (*This is intended for married couples.*)
14. *Madena Sohon Bandenay.*—Quarrelling—hating each other—insanity—sores and boils at the joints—paralytic attacks of rheumatism—divers diseases. (*Intended against married couples.*)
15. *Gadewara Iripenneema.*—Madness—running into woods, graveyards, and streams—shouting—dancing—extreme heat in the blood—speedy death.
16. *Golu Keelay.*—Dumbness.
17. *Madena Sangilla Tatuwa.*—Cough and consumption—itching pain over the skin—insanity.

L

18. *Wandi Bandu Jeewama.*—A man cannot remain in his house—he must run away from it.

19. *Ratnimiti Well Penneema.*—Death in seven days.

20. *Wijja Paluwa.*—A man forgets all that he knew of any science or art.

21. *Kamuruwa.*—If you pronounce the charm over some water, and sprinkle it on a person's hand, the latter will fall down on the ground.

22. *Reeri Kamuruwa.*—The same effects as the above, with this addition, that the man who falls will bleed through the nose.

23. *Oddi Reeri Dæhenay.*—Fever—paralysis—rheumatic pains—sores and boils—death in three years.

24. *Cal-lu Carpuwa.*—Immediate death.

25. *Jala Rama Bandenay.*—Rheumatic attacks—death within three months.

The following is the Hooniyan charm called Cadewara Iripenneema (No. 15 in the above list.)

"Adored be thou, Oh Buddha! The she-demons Cadawara Reeri Yaksenee, Billey Reeri Yaksenee, Calu Candi Yaksenee, Marana Keela Yaksenee, Samayan Cadawara Reeri Yaksenee, and Calu Roopa Yaksenee, who all sprang into being from the blood, which spouted up into the air from the heart of queen Seetapatee of the city Seetapatee Nuvera, once upon a time rushed into Bangala (Bengal) and thence to Nuvera Ellia, where they rested on the rock Gala Tala (Pedro Talla Galla.) Each wore around her neck a garland of flowers, a chain of gold, and a chain of silver. They then sent forth a deadly ball of fire and smoke to Ramapura, and another to prince Rama, by which both that prince and the prince Sumana Disti Cumara were affected with demon-influence. Next they looked down upon the rest of the world of human beings, and took possession of 1000 children, 1000 women, and 1000 men, making these creatures tremble, and cry, and shout, and rave, and die. These she-demons I bind by the power of the king Wissamonny. Let the she-demons Muni Cadawara Reeri Yaksanee,

Yamacali Yaksenee, Raticami Yaksenee, and Sanni Cami Yaksenee, come hither. Come instantly. Come, thundering from the sky. Make the sky and the earth roar and reel, as ye come. The she-demons Cadawara Reeri Yaksenee and Muni Billey Yaksenee with others once went to the city Capila, and began to devour the citizens; whereupon the king Wissamonny and the king of the gods, binding them with chains of fire and human bones, checked their ferocity and frightened them exceedingly. Therefore by the power of these gods, I command you, oh she-demons, to look here. I command you to come directly to me without looking anywhere else. I bow down to thee, Oh Buddha! The she-demons Lay Cadawara Yaksenee, Reeri Cadawara Yaksenee, and Aawey Cadawara Yaksenee once went to the mountain Nawasiagiri Parwatte, where they devoured the heads of nine hundred princes, and killed the great prince Cewulia Cumara, whose blood they drank. When the son of king Wijeyo was playing in his royal father's flower garden, Aaweysa Cadawara Reeri Yaksenee struck him with her necklace of flowers, which hurled him many thousand fathoms high into the air. She once went to the rock Maha Lay Parwatte, but the great demon chief Malla told her to descend to the earth inhabited by men, and to feed on such as she liked. Oh Aaweysa Cadawara Reeri Yaksenee, I call upon thee to listen to what thy priest tells thee. Demon, thy own priest calls upon thee. I beg thee to attend to what I tell thee, and not to any thing else, which any other priest may tell thee. Oh Aaweysa Cadawara Reeri Yaksenee, oh great she-demon, I call upon thee this day to be bound by my charm. I call upon thee to accept an offering, which I make to thee and thy sisters. I call upon thee by the power of all the gods. Therefore, come here. Look here and come soon. I call upon thee, and command thee by the power of Vishnu, to cast thy influence upon this human being, and to take him wholly to thyself. I beg thee to protect me. I call upon thee to tell thee, that from this day, and this hour, and this minute this human sacrifice, which I dedicate to thee, is wholly thine. The Cattadiyas are thy obedient slaves. Therefore protect me, but take this human being as an offering acceptable to thee. Take him. Take him this instant as an offering made by thy servant. Oh she-demon, oh my sister, eat him. Eat his flesh and drink his blood. Eat his bones, and muscles, and nerves. Drink his heart's blood and suck his marrow. Eat his liver and lungs and entrails. Look at him from head to toe, and cover him this instant with thy influence. I command thee this day, oh Aaweysa Cadawara, Reeri Yaksanee, who wast born from three drops of blood, to suck the blood out of this human being. I give him over to thee. Take him. I ask thee and all other she-demons to afflict him with heat, fever, and pain in all the 800 joints and 900 nerves of his body, and in the 300,000,000 pores of his skin. Remain thou with him, till I come back to thee. I tell thee, listen not to any other Cattadiya. By Wissamonny's power I bind thee to do this. I bind thee. I have bound thee. Let this be so.'

The Jeewama of the above—"Make three *Pidayni Tatu* (altárs) and divide each Tatuwa into four compartments. Place in each of these compartments boiled rice of a yellow colour, some of a white colour, and some of a black colour; also place on any of the Tatu some milk in two separate leaves, some blood in two separate leaves, five kinds of fried meat, an arrow, and a cock. Surround all these with three turns of a Kan-ya Nool thread. Then placing one of the Tatu to the east of you, and the other two at your feet, pronounce the charm 133 times over a Kan-ya Nool thread and a cluster of Rat Mal flowers, which you hold in your hand.* You will then see three apparitions, but, without getting frightened by them, bind them by your charm. Then take away the thread and the flowers, and get them *passed over:* after which, keep them carefully secured in a box. This Jeewama must be performed on a grave during three Yamas of a Sunday. The man will get mad in three days."

* The *dummala* incense, although not mentioned above, must also be used on this and on all similar occasions. It is omitted here, only because it is too well known as a *sine qua non* of every demon ceremony to require express mention.

The Jeewama of *Sohon Gini Bandenay* (No. 13 in the above list)—"Near a tree, the bark of which has much sap in it, draw on the ground two figures representing the man and his wife, with a piece of charcoal obtained from a place where a human corpse had been burned. Write the names of the parties on the breasts of these figures with the same piece of charcoal. Write also on each of the figures the letters *a. e. u.* Then pronounce the charm over a steel nail, and drive the nail into those parts of the figures which represent the private parts. Pronounce the charm again over 16 nails made of *Pas lo,* and drive them into those parts of the figures which represent the joints. Remove then the earth on which the figures were drawn, and bury it in a grave a few inches below the surface, and make a fire over it with *Pas Pengiri* (the wood of five kinds of trees the fruit of which is sour to the taste:) Keep up this fire for sometime. For offerings, put on an altar some blood, some Rat Mal flowers, a roasted egg, and some boiled rice, each in a separate leaf. All this must be done on a Sunday. The husband and wife will fall sick, become insane, have paralysis in their legs, quarrel and fight with each other, and die at the end of three months, if remedies are not applied in time. The remedy is this—dig a hole in the ground where a human corpse has been burnt. Throw in it nine kinds of flowers and some boiled rice, each folded in 9 separate leaves. Put on an altar close by 9 leaves containing the juice of Rat Mal flowers, and 9 containing boiled rice, and 8 limes. Repeat then these charms (not given here), and taking the limes to the sick people, cut them, pronouncing over them the seven charms *Hanama Wettu Alagu.* The sick people will recover."

The Jeewama of *Madena Sohon Bandenay* (No. 14)—"Draw the figure of a man on a tiger's skin, and the figure of a woman on a deer skin. Write the names of the man and his wife on the breasts of the respective figures. Then put upon the figures a *Divi Caduru* leaf,* a piece of charcoal obtained from a funeral

* *Divi Caduru* is a tree which grows to a considerable height. Its leaves are about a foot long, and two and a half or three inches broad, very thick,

pile, and seven grains of unboiled rice. Fold these in the skins, and tie the two skins together with seven turns of a Kan-ya Nool thread. Before you use the thread for this purpose, repeat over it this charm 49 times, taking care to make a knot every seventh time. Then take 9 thorns from Pas Pengiri trees, and pronouncing the charm 9 times over them drive them into the skins. Make also an altar, and place upon it Rat Mal flowers, milk, porri, and sandal wood, each in a separate leaf, place these at the four corners of the altar, and the skins in the middle. Then perfume them with the smoke of resin, and pronounce the charm 7 times. All this must be done on a Sunday during the morning Yama. After this take away the skins and strike with them the stone, which is opposite to the door of the house. The man and his wife will become insane, and quarrel with each other, and die in a short time."

Every Hooniyan, that produces sickness, ends in death, unless it is prevented in time by charms; and no other remedy but charms can effect a cure, whatever the nature of the disease may be. The longer the Hooniyan influence remains on a man, the less chance there is of its removal, probably because the demon acquires a sort of prescriptive right over his victim, until he bring the man to death in his own time, that is within the time assigned in the charm. Hence, in the mind of a Singhalese, suspicion is always awake and ready to discover a Hooniyan cause in the various misfortunes, which he may meet with in the ordinary course of nature, in the form of disease and accidents. And hence also it is, that he so often has recourse to charms and demon ceremonies, even when he is in the enjoyment of perfectly good health, merely because he wants to ease his mind, which otherwise would be made very unhappy by a doubt, whether a Hooniyan influence may not then be upon him, although as yet there does not appear even to himself any thing, which he can consider to be a sign of it.

---

and of a dark green colour. When bent, the leaf breaks and exudes a thick white sap considered to be poisonous. The fruit when ripe is of a beautiful red colour, and is very tempting to the sight, from which circumstance probably it is, that it has sometimes been called *Eve's Apple.*

Angam Charms.

There is another class of charms, which, though intended to injure others like Hooniyan, have yet been called by a different name, and are supposed to have been originated by a different Irshi. While Hooniyans are supposed to affect a man at different intervals, varying from a day to 30 or 40 years from the time of the Jeewama, and to cause death generally by slow degrees, preceded by a variety of diseases, of which insanity, paralysis in the limbs, and extreme heat in the region of the chest are the most common; these are supposed to be more speedy in their effects, death taking place invariably within seven hours, without any previous indication of disease other than a throwing up of blood through the nose and mouth. These charms are called Angams, of which there are onl· 32. The following are their names:—

1 Udatringey Angam
2 Hasta Angam
3 Suruttu Angam
4 Talpat Angam
5 Neecha Cula Angam
6 Rodi Angam
7 Caturu Angam
8 Leynsu Angam
9 Tadicara Angam
10 Choragata Angam
11 Reeri Angam
12 Hanuma Angam
13 Heywa Yakse Angam
14 Hena Rawana Angam
15 Maha Sohon Angam
16 Muduhiru Angam
17 Narapura Induwa
18 Narapura Inchia
19 Naraporottuwa
20 Widurucodi Angam
21 Widuru Maraney
22 Geri Angam
23 Hasti Angam
24 Cula Angam
25 Sunaka Angam
26 Taruka Angam
27 Yakse Angam
28 Wata Angam
29 Curumbera Angam
30 Raja Angam
31 Dewa Angam
32 Neela Angam

These Angams are made use of in the following manner. After the jeewama, the substance subjected to that ceremony, whether it be a flower, a thread, an image, a stick, a handkerchief, a finger ring, or a young cocoanut leaflet, is sometimes (1) buried in the ground at some place, which the intended victim may happen to "pass over" as in Hooniyan; or (2) the operator may keep it in his hand and blow upon it, so as to make the breath fall upon him, or (3) he may touch his person with it still holding it in his hand, or (4) he may throw it into his face, or (5) he may fan him with it, or (6) he may make him touch it, or (7) he may leave it at some particular place, where he cannot but take it when he sees it, or (8) he may stretch out his hand towards him, or (9) he may keep it in his hand, and only look at his face: which of these is to be done, depends upon the nature of the particular Angam. In almost all these cases, the victim is supposed to fall down suddenly in a state of insensibility and to bleed, profusely from the nose and mouth, and, if remedies are not applied within seven hours, death is said to be the result.

Udatringey Angam (No. 1 in the List,) is to be used against a man who happens to be standing on any thing higher than the ground, as for instance on a tree, for it is supposed that none of the other Angams can produce any effect on him, so long as he does not touch the ground with his feet. It is also thought that those sailing on water can be affected only by this, but on this point the scientific in these matters do not seem to be agreed.

In the next, No. 2, the charm is pronounced over the right hand' which then, being extended towards any one, is supposed to make him fall, bleeding from his nose and mouth, and death ensues at the end of seven hours.

In No. 3, a quantity of *Rat Mal* flowers, over which the charm has been duly pronounced at the Jeewama, are rolled up with tobacco into a cigar, which is smoked, so as to let the smoke be blown by the wind towards another. The same consequences follow as in the 1st.

In No. 4, an Ola being charmed is rolled up in the form of a *Talpotta* or native Ola letter, * and is sent to the party marked

* *Talpotta* is the leaf of the Palmyra, as *Talapotta* is of the Talipot. The leaf of the Palmyra was, a few years back, the "Note" and "Letter" paper of the Natives; and it is still so generally throughout the Island. The leaf of the Talipot is seldom used for this purpose, but is reserved for making books.

for destruction, who, on breaking open or rather unloosing the bands of what appears to him to be a letter, falls down senseless.

If a man however be fortified by charms against Angams and other agents of demoniac power, he can be affected only by the Angam called *Neecha Cula Angam*, (No. 5), which can break through all such defences, and affect the man as easily as if he had never been protected by any charms whatever.

If you tell a Cattadiya that his science of charms is nothing but an absurd ridiculous fiction, calculated to delude only the most ignorant and credulous; that it can do nothing to those who do not believe in it, and if you ask him why it can not injure an Englishman, although the latter courts and challenges a trial, he will tell you, if you are a Singhalese, (but if you are an Englishman, he will give you a very different reason), that, though a demon revels in blood and human carcasses, yet he possesses certain ideas of cleanliness and decency, and that therefore he is unwilling to affect with his influence an Englishman, who does not cleanse his person with water after the discharge of the bodily functions; he will tell you indeed that there is *one low filthy demon*, who, being indifferent to dirt, does influence even an Englishman, *when forced to it* by the charm called *Rodi Angam*, (No. 6); but that in the Jeewama of this Angam, a green leaf of the *Alu Kesel** plantain tree, used by a *Rodia* (a man of the lowest caste in the Island) to put his meals on, is necessary; and that it is extremely difficult to get this, as no Rodia will leave it behind him after he has taken his meals on it, and will not part with it to any but one of his own caste.

If sticks or clubs, submitted to the Jeewama of *Tadicara Angam* (No. 9), are left on roads and other places frequented by people, any person passing by and seeing them will be irresistibly compelled to take them up, and use them in assaulting every one he may happen to see, and at last turn them against himself.

---

* *Alu Kesel* literally means *Ash* Plantain; it is so called from its fruit being covered with something similar to ashes.

The following is the charm *Neela Angam* (No. 32):—

"Oh Brahma, Vishnu, and Siva, may you be adored! Oh demon of blood, receive this human sacrifice, which I make to thee. Accept it instantly. Look at it with thy thousand eyes. Oh Brahma, Vishnu, and Siva, may you be adored! Stop ye, Pilliran and Neeliran. Wissamonny's power is great. There is not a demon, who does not feel his power. Stop thou, Caluga Pullay! Vishnu is great. His authority prevails over all demons. Stop thou, Elendri Dewi! Stop ye all! I make this sacrifice to you. I dedicate this human being to you. Blood of a delicious taste, heart, lungs, liver, and marrow, all delicious, are yours. I deliver him to you. Take charge of him. He is yours. Thou, Reeri Yaksanee, look at him instantly, and take him as an offering acceptable to thee. Take him immediately. Throw him down. Oh Brahma, Vishnu, and Siva, adoration be to you! The powers which originated from queen Yasodara, and the powers belonging to Vishnu, as they now prevail at the temple of the Cannibal demons, and who once destroyed the prince Wisamatoma—by these powers I deliver this being to thy charge, Oh Siddhi Maha Sohon dewatawa, and to thy charge, thou son of Gajacumbacari. By those powers I command, that he, who crosses this stile before my return hither, be taken charge of by Billey Gopolu Yaksanee. Let the dewatawa [Maha Sohona] take charge of him, as his. Let Billey dewatawa of the South take charge of him, as his. Let Dalla Seyna, chief of demons, take charge of him, as his. Take him. Thou Siddhi Maha Sohon dewatawa, look at him and take him. Throw him down. Throw him. Do it. Let this be so."

The Jeewama of the above—"Make a Mal Bulat Tatuwa on a grave, or at a place where three paths meet, and put on it some sandal wood dissolved in water, a few Rat Mal, Idda Mal, and Jessamine flowers, each kind in a separate leaf. Make a Pidayni Tatuwa* and put upon it a human bone, some porri, a little blood,

* The difference between a Mal Bulat Tatuwa and a Pidyani Tatuwa is, that on the former rice and other eatables are not offered, while on the latter they are, with or without flowers and perfumes.

and the fang of a Cobra de Capello, each in separate leaves, together with a young king cocoanut cut open at one end without spilling its water. Then surround the whole with a Kan-ya Nool thread, so as to include within the ring the Mal Bulat Tatuwa, Pidayni Tatuwa, and yourself. Lie down on your back with your head towards the north. Place one of the Tatus on your right and the other on your left, and the fire pot and resin near your right foot. Repeat then the charm 108 times, each time smoking the two Tatus with the resin. Do this during the midnight Yama of a Sunday. After this, put the sandal wood powder carefully into a little box, and pronouncing over it the charm three times, shut the lid with your right hand, while you support the box on the back of your left hand. Then take this away, and rub some of the sandal powder on any of the cross sticks of the fence stile with the middle finger of your right hand; every one, who attempts to get over that stile during the first seven hours, commencing from the time you first rubbed the sandal on it, will fall down senseless and bleeding, and, if not cured immediately, will die in seven hours."

Angams and Wedding processions are so intimately connected with each other in the mind of a Singhalese, that, if a bridegroom or his bride happen to feel a little unwell while on their way to be married, it will most probably be attributed to an Angam. During these processions, that is, when the bridegroom goes to the house of the bride, or when he returns to his own accompanied by her and all their relatives, it sometimes happens, that either he or she, and sometimes both, get hysterical and fall into swoons which last about a quarter of an hour. This is most probably owing to their having, for the best part of the day, been obliged to remain overloaded with an amount of clothing,* to which they (especially the

* The ordinary dress of a man of the middle classes consists only of a *Saron* or four yards of white cloth, wrapped round his person so as to cover it from the waist to a little below the knee. When a man has occasion to go beyond the precincts of his village, this dress is a little improved upon ; he puts on a jacket and sometimes a shirt and wears sandals on his feet, he adorns his head too with a large comb, which is worn in different fashions by different castes.

man) had never been accustomed; combined with the heat, noise, excitement, and their own consciousness of being for the time the "observed of all observers." Hysterics or any sudden sickness on such occasions is always attributed to an Angam caused by some unfriendly person among the company. The Cattadiya, who often forms one of the company to be ready on such an emergency to render his services, does his part on such an occasion, and of course the patient generally recovers under his management, as much to the glory and honour of the profession as to his own personal benefit. I recollect several instances of this kind, which have occurred in my own presence, among others, the following:—

About 19 years ago, when I was a lad of 15, I was on my way to school with three or four school fellows, when we heard the usual accompaniment of a Wedding Procession, viz., the sound of drums and of brass cymbals, mingled with the loud voices of three or four singing men all chanting together in a sort of chorus. We all stopped to see the procession, which was slowly moving on towards us at some distance in our rear; and as their way lay in the same direction and on the same road as ours, we gladly kept them company, keeping as near as possible to the tom-tom players and the dancing boys, who interested us much more than anybody else in the procession, the bride and bridegroom included. Immediately behind us were some 10 or 15 people, and next to them came the bridegroom. He was dressed, as is usual on such an occasion, in the style of a Modliar, and was attended on his right and left by his two "friends," men nearly of the same stature and dressed in the same style as* himself. Then came some more people, and behind them the bride and another woman in a bullock *hackery*. Scarcely ten minutes had elapsed from the time we joined them, when we heard the cry *apoyi* (alas), the usual expression of distress. I turned round, and saw the bridegroom with closed eyes and drops of perspiration pouring down his face in the

* Instead of men of the same height as the bridegroom sometimes two little boys are substituted, which custom however prevails only in and near the larger towns.

arms of three or four people, who were supporting him from falling down, and apparently senseless. His great velvet coat was now removed, and the shirt collar opened to give him the benefit of air. In another moment a man was seen pronouncing in an inaudible voice (the motion of the lips alone could be seen) his charms, first over a lock of hair of the sick man, which he formed into a knot after his mutterings were concluded, and then over a cup of water. In 5 or 6 minutes more, some of the charmed water was sprinkled over the man's face, and some poured down his throat. He almost immediately recovered, and the procession again moved on. When the incantations were over, I heard the Cattadiya say, with an air of confidence and triumph. "Now, don't fear, he will be all right soon," and sure enough he was, which even then, young as I was, I thought was more owing to the refreshing coolness of the water he drank, than to any supernatural virtues imparted to it by the incantations. Several members of the procession, especially the nearest relatives of the bridegroom, gave vent to their feelings of resentment in dark, mysterious hints, expressed in obscure and sententious language, such as "Very well" with a peculiar shake of the head, "Well, let us see," "You can see," "We are also still living," and other similar expressions, quite intelligible to a Singhalese, and which boded no good to the culprit, who had brought this Angam on the bridegroom.

We can adduce instances like this in great numbers; but the above will suffice to give an idea of a Wedding procession afflicted by what is supposed to be an Angam charm.

In 99 cases out of a hundred, it is the bride, and not the bridegroom, who displays these symptoms of what is supposed to be Angam influence.

Whether a Cattadiya forms one of the procession or not, certain precautions are always taken against the bridegroom or the bride falling under the influence of an Angam. These precautions consist in pronouncing charms over one end of the handkerchief which they carry in their hands, and then tying up that end into a knot. Sometimes other amulets called *Yantra* are worn about their persons.

There are three other kinds of charms, called respectively KALAN, CULAMBU, and SERRA, intended for the same purpose, and used nearly in the same manner as Angams, but slightly differing from them in certain respects. This difference is said to consist in this, viz., that, while Angams can only affect men, Kalang, Culambu, and Serra are powerful enough to affect demons too, although in their case death does not result, as in the case of men. These are said to be used sometimes in cases of demoniac possession, when it is found difficult to exorcise the demon by ordinary charms. The exact number of these has not been ascertained. We give below the names of some of them.

Calang.

1. Vishnu Calang	4. Pattini Calang
2. Canda Cumara Calang	5. Dewol Calang
3. Dedimunda Calang	6. Narapura Calang.

Culambu.

1. Vishnu Culambu	4. Pattini Culambu
2. Canda Cumara Culambu	5. Dewol Culambu
3. Dedi Munda Culambu	

Serra.

1. Vishnu Serra	4. Pattini Serra
2. Canda Cumara Serra	5. Dewol Serra
3. Dedi Munda Serra	6. Wayissrawana Serra.

The Jeewama of these three classes of charms is supposed to be attended with greater danger to those engaged in it, than of any other class of charms yet mentioned, and it is pretended that on that account they are seldom or never resorted to.

PILLI CHARMS.

We now come to that, which is considered to be the highest and most important class of charms, which is said to exhibit the extraordinary powers of the art of Sorcery in the most unequivocal manner. We mean *Pilli*. In the case of the other classes of charms already noticed, although the effects produced by them are brought about by demons, yet these demons themselves, never appear visibly to men even in disguise, except at the Jeewama ceremony of some of them. But the Pilli charms are considered to be so singularly powerful, that the demons assume some visible shape, while executing the duty assigned them by the charm. Besides, the effects of a Pilli charm are said to be instantaneous, almost simultaneous with the conclusion of the Jeewama. In the case of Hooniyan (a very few excepted), several months may elapse before the charm begins to take effect, and even then it takes a considerable time to bring the man to his grave. In Angams there is an interval of seven hours between the moment of death and the time, when the charm first takes effect. But in Pilli, death is the only effect, and that almost simultaneous with the Jeewama. Again, both in Hooniyans and Angams, even after they have taken effect, there is still a chance of a cure at any time before the man breathes his last; but the moment a Pilli charm takes effect, there is an end of every hope of escape, even though the actual moment of death may be an hour or two later. If a man however be a sorcerer himself, and, *before* the charm has taken effect on him, is able to ascertain that a Pilli is directed against him, he can, if he is acquainted with the necessary counter charms, ward off the danger, provided he immediately does what is necessary. There are eighteen different Pillis, of which Cumara Pilli is the most popular. We give below the names of these 18. They are as follows:—

1. Reeri Pilli
2. Naga Pilli
3. Cumara Pilli
4. Coli Pilli
5. Kan-ya Pilli
6. Kana Mediri Pilli
7. Garunda Pilli
8. Curumini Pilli
9. Mala Pilli
10. Maha Sohon Pilli
11. Oddi Pilli
12. Debara Pilli
13. Bambara Pilli
14. Widiga Pilli
15. Singha Pilli
16. Gaja Pilli
17. Gini Pilli
18. Neecha Cula Pilli.

In each of these a particular demon is supposed to go to the intended victim, disguised in some particular form. In the first he is said to disguise himself as a fair looking young man; in the second, as a Cobra de Capello; in the third, as a boy; in the fourth, as a hen; in the fifth, as a little girl; in the sixth, as a firefly; in the seventh, as a peacock; in the eighth, as a beetle; in the ninth, as an old man; in the tenth, as a wild hog; in the eleventh, as an old woman; in the twelfth, as a hornet; in the thirteenth, as a bee; in the fourteenth, as a Malabar man; in the fifteenth, as a lion; in the sixteenth, as an elephant; in the seventeenth, as a ball of fire; and in the eighteenth, as a dog.

Soon after the approach of the demon, the man is said suddenly to drop down dead, or to vomit blood first and die immediately afterwards. In some Pillis the demon uses violence, and either stabs the man, or strangles him to death. In the preparation of Cumara Pilli, the corpse of a male infant, the firstborn of his mother, is essential. This is first submitted to a sort of embalming process, and then having been dried by the heat of a fire made with sandal and Pas Pengiri wood, is locked up in a box made of *Cohomba* or Banyan wood, and placed in some spot unfrequented by women, so as to be safe from the pollution of *Kili* or Uncleanness.* At the Jeewama, two knives are placed in its right and left hands, and the charm is then pronounced over it, during the three Yamas of a Sunday, on a grave not more than three days old. Of course, offerings are made to the demons, as usual. It is supposed that

* The *Uncleanness*, or as it is called in Singhalese *Kili*, is a sort of imaginary pollution anxiously avoided in every thing relating to Demon Worship. The principal occasions or causes of uncleanness are the death of a human being, the menstrual discharge in women, the flesh of certain animals such as pigs, peacocks, monkeys, and the fishes *Magura* and *Ingura*, and the birth of a child. In the case of death, the uncleanness is supposed to last for three months together; and it extends its mysterious influence not only in and near the dead body or the house where the man died, but to a distance of "seven gardens" [about a ¼ or ¾ of a mile] from that house. The uncleanness arising from death is the most malignant, and is supposed to come upon a person, even when he passes by the house of a deceased person. The principal consequence

demons then come in great numbers to the scene, endeavouring in every possible manner to frighten away the men, who however take care before the commencement of the ceremony to fortify themselves by charms and other amulets against these attacks. When the charm is perfected, the mummy becomes animated, and stands up. Then, certain other charms being pronounced over it, the name of the intended victim written on an ola is tied round its neck or its wrist; it then flies through the air like lightning to the man, who is to be destroyed. If the latter happen to be himself a man well learned in charms of this description, and if he recognize the disguised demon instantly, he will be able by means of certain other charms to send back the demon, who, when so sent, will and must kill the person, who first roused him at the Jeewama, no charm nor amulet of any kind being of any avail against him on this occasion. But if the former fail to pronounce his charm, either from not knowing one, or through fright, or from not suspecting a Pilli demon in the animal before him, it will be all over with him in a short time, no charms or any other demon ceremonies whatever helping him in the least, after the Pilli has once taken effect, that effect being generally immediate death.

If you ask a Cattadiya or any other Singhalese, who is at all conversant with these matters, whether these Pilli charms are actually put in practice now, and whether they are really followed by the wonderful results ascribed to them, he will first consider you, if a Singhalese, to be a fellow spoiled by contamination with Englishmen or by your English education, and then tell you that

---

of exposing oneself to the influence of this Uncleanness, is sickness, and in the case of a man, who is already suffering from some sickness, the consequence will be to aggravate the disease. A man bitten by a mad dog, if exposed accidentally to this influence within three months, is supposed to get hydrophobia, and die most miserably. Hence this Uncleanness is greatly dreaded by the people, and none but the very nearest relatives will enter the garden of a house in which a person has died, the more distant relatives remaining outside the garden fence.

at present the science is on the decline, that now there are few or none skilful enough to be able to perform those charms without danger to themselves, and that therefore instances of Pilli charms successfully performed in these degenerate days, are not so general as those of Hooniyan charms, but that the science itself is as true, as that Buddha was the greatest being that ever was born in the world. He will confirm this statement by regaling you with a hundred anecdotes, how such and such a Pilli had succeeded at such and such a place, with all the interesting particulars connected with them. If you shew any symptoms of scepticism about the accuracy of his marvellous accounts, he will endeavour to remove all your doubts and scruples, by giving you the benefit of his own experience of a certain Pilli charm, which actually killed, or was very nearly killing, an acquaintance or relative of his.

The following is an anecdote of this kind, which we give in the words of the narrator :—

"Well, Sir," said he, "you must freely pardon me, when I tell you that young men—I beg your pardon again and again, Sir, for saying so—know very little about these matters. You think—pray, don't be angry with me for saying so—that all that is great and wonderful is peculiar to the European. You have been taught to read English books and to imbibe from them notions, which militate both against the faith of our forefathers, and against the illustrious sciences they cultivated. This unnatural conduct has in some instances been pursued so far, as even to make some of our young men cut their hair and put on trowsers. Long hair and the *Condey,** which have so long been the pride and honourable badges of our nation, are now despised by some of these young men, as if they were marks of degradation. Instead of combs, they now wear English *Piriwehi*† on their heads. But alas! there is

---

* *Condey* is the hair tied up into a knot behind the head.

† *Piriwehi* is a basket made of cocoanut leaflets for some temporary purpose, and it is sometimes used derisively as a contemptuous nickname for a cap or hat.

no help, no remedy for all this. Well, Sir, you speak of the omnipotence of English science as being able to send news by an iron rod thousands of miles in a few minutes, to make carriages loaded with 70 or 100 cart-loads of goods move at the rate of 30 or 40 miles an hour merely by the agency of fire and smoke, without the help of bullocks or horses. You speak of English medicine as being superior to our medicine. But do you know, Sir, that none of these sciences or arts originally belonged to the Englishman himself. They all belonged formerly to Brahmins, and the English or some other Europeans have somehow or other met with their books; and, because they are men of sense and thought, they have been able to apply the rules laid down in those books to something practical, by which they may advance their interests. The Brahmins may not perhaps have those books with them now; but even if they have, they neither possess the opportunities, nor the means, nor even the energy and grasp of mind, necessary to derive any practical benefit from them, like the English." He went on in this manner for a full hour, and then continued, "To remove then every doubt from your mind respecting Pilli, I will tell you what happened once under my own eye. One day about 25 years ago, my eldest brother had a quarrel about some charm-books with a native of the Matura district, who was then a guest at the house of a neighbour. Of course, after the quarrel, which was confined only to words, we thought no more of it. About 12 o'clock the following night, there came into the Verandah of my brother's house, where I happened to be that night, a hen with a large brood of chickens. I was awake, though my brother was fast asleep. Of course to my mind there was nothing extraordinary in the matter, but the next moment my brother awoke, exclaiming in a very loud voice 'Chee! Chee,!' and then told me in* a hurried manner to bring him a few grains of rice. Though I was surprised both by his exclamation and by his excited manner, I obeyed and immedi-

---

* *Chee* is an Interjection expressive of disgust or contempt, and is nearly equivalent to the English *Pshaw*.

ately brought him a handful of rice from a Chatty* in the kitchen opposite, wondering all the while what my brother was going to do. He took the rice into his hand, and muttering a charm over it threw it to the hen, which during this time, which was not more than 4 or 5 minutes altogether, was moving round and round my brother's bed. The hen first fluttered its wings, and then very quickly picked up the grains and went away, all the while croaking and cackling in a peculiar way. My brother then shewed me a small piece of flesh looking like the heart of a fowl, still dripping with blood, which, he said, fell on his breast and roused him from sleep; this was the *Coli Pilli* (No. 4 in the list); and he congratulated himself on his narrow escape, and on his success in turning back the Pilli to the very man, who had sent it to him. Well, Sir, the next morning we heard that the Matura man had died during the night, Well, now, what say you to that?" Knowing very well that the greatest miracle, that could be performed in these modern times, would be to convince by reasoning an uneducated old Singhalese of the absurdity of any of his opinions, we contented ourselves with quietly remarking, "that it appeared to us, that, without the agency of a Pilli or any other charm, it was quite possible that a hen and its chickens should come into an open Verandah, also carrying with it a piece of flesh picked up somewhere; that it was equally possible that the hen should, while moving about the bed, drop the piece of flesh on the man sleeping on it; and that it was not at all miraculous that a neighbour, with whom your brother may have had a quarrel lately, should die by some natural means the same night." On this, the old man looked daggers at us, but suppressing his rage he replied, "but I was wide awake, and saw the hen from the first moment she came into the Verandah to the moment of her leaving it, and during all that time I did not see her getting on the bed or dropping a piece of flesh on my brother's person." "Could not the hen have come

* *Chatty* is the name given to any earthen vessel of a moderate size used as cooking utensil.

into the Verandah," said we, "sometime before you awoke, and have left the flesh on your brother's person without either of you being aware of it at the time; and could not the hen then have returned to the Verandah a second time, the time that you say you saw her coming in." "Nonsense, that was not possible," said he, "for the moment the piece of flesh fell on my brother's person, he called out, as I said before; and it was the fall of the lump of flesh that roused him. Sir, I am sorry you should thus cavil at things which our forefathers believed, and which we old folks have ourselves found to be as true now, as they were in the days of the Irshis." The old man seemed very excited, and the more untenable any of his arguments appeared even to himself, the more dogmatic and wrathful he got. When any of his statements or arguments appeared to admit of explanation on ordinary reasonable grounds, he was sure to oppose it by advancing a fact or two, for which, we are quite sure, he was more beholden to his imagination and invention than to his memory. This old man is a respectable man in his own way, has had all the advantages of education according to the native system, and is a type of a large class of the Singhalese. What those say or think, who are still less enlightened, and who have not had the same "advantages of education," the reader may easily imagine.

During a previous part of our conversation on the same subject, he told us another anecdote of the same kind, which he had *heard* from a "trustworthy" person. "Some 25 or 30 years ago," said he, "there was a man named Abileenu, a boutique-keeper in the town of Kandy. Among other things exposed for sale in his boutique, there were some green *Aanamalu* plantains.* Another man named Bayi Appoo came to this boutique one day, and wish-

---

* *Aanamalu* is a kind of plantain very common in Ceylon ; the fruit is longer than in any other species, and is used by the Singhalese in curries. All other kinds of plantain, when quite ripe, acquire a reddish colour, especially in their outer coverings, but Aanamalu alone always retains, even when ripe, the same green colour, that it had before it had become ripe.

ing to buy some of the plantains enquired their price; on being told that eight were sold for a *pice*,* he offered to buy twelve for a *pice*, which so irritated Abileenu, that he abused the other in very indecent language, using among other expressions this—'send your mother to me with a bag to fetch plantains at twelve for a pice.' Well, Bayi Appoo, who had only done what any other man would have done when he wanted to buy any article from a boutique, was very much provoked by this language, which he had not deserved; therefore when he heard the expression "Send your mother to me with a bag to fetch plantains at twelve for a pice," he rushed towards the other intending to box his ears, but suddenly checking himself he replied "very well, then I will send her to you to-night," and he went away. That night about 12 o'clock there came to Abileenu's boutique an old gray-haired woman. How she got in after the doors had been fast locked, was more than Abileenu's people could say. But there she was, sitting on a bag and looking steadfastly with glowing fiery eyes at the sleeping Abileenu. In a very short time Abileenu was heard to utter a loud, shrill scream, and the next morning after daylight when the other people of the boutique looked at Abileenu, they found him a cold corpse. One of these boutique people himself told me all this."

About eight years ago, the death of a young woman from the bite of a Cobra in a village not far from Caltura was attributed to a Pilli; to prove that it was so, her relatives argued that, although death may follow the bite of a Cobra without there being any Pilli in the matter, yet in this particular instance the snake, which could have bitten many other people who were more in its way, purposely avoided them all; and that, although many attempted to drive it away from the neighbourhood of the house, yet it did not only not leave the premises, but ran through the midst of the other people, until it approached the young woman, and fastened its fatal fangs in her.

---

* A *pice* is three-eighths of a penny.

Some five or six years ago, a man was killed by a wild hog, while he was sitting near his own door in a distant part of Hewagam Corle; and because this happened in broad daylight at his own house, it was attributed to a Pilli caused by an enemy with the assistance of some Cattadiya.

JEEWANG, BANDENA, AND DEHENA CHARMS.

JEEWANG is the name of a particular class of charms, whose object is to "bind" any demon in a certain manner to the will of a man, so as to make him an obedient slave to the latter, whether he wishes him to inflict sickness or to perform ordinary domestic work. In all other charms a demon has only to execute a particular duty on one particular occasion or during a certain length of time, and, when that is done, he is free; but in Jeewang Charms the demon becomes a perpetual slave, and ceases to be a free agent, as far as the man, who has bound him, is concerned. The following are the names of a few of these charms:—

1. Aacora Jeewama
2. Mohanee Jeewama
3. Irala Jeewama
4. Oddiya Jeewama
5. Bahirawa Jeewama
6. Saraspatee Jeewama
7. Aananda Bahirawa Jeewama
8. Maha Bahirawa Jeewama
9. Patthracali Jeewama
10. Hanuma Jeewama

A demon, who is under the influence of these charms, is supposed to be always in the company of the man, never being able to leave him for a moment, or to disobey him in any thing, until the death of the latter dissolve the bond. He travels with the man, sits wherever he sits, waits near his bed when he sleeps, and is his constant companion. He does every thing his master commands, whether it be the infliction of death, or drawing water from wells, or repairing the garden fence, or removing heavy stones which had resisted the united exertions of hundreds of men, or felling large trees, or doing any thing else desired by his master. A man, who has a demon under his control in this manner, is therefore supposed to be a dangerous neighbour, for his power is considered to be such, that, even when he speaks to or looks at another angrily, the latter is supposed to fall sick. Such a man is supposed to have a very disagreeable exterior, seldom combing his hair or washing his person, and looking generally sulky and stern; ungracious in his manner, soon put out of temper, and avoiding pork and other things considered to be unclean. He is also scrupulous in avoiding houses or other places contaminated by any Uncleanness.

This sort of close connection with a demon is however considered to be very dangerous,in as much as the demon, though paying an unwilling and forced obedience to the man, is yet always watching for an opportunity of destroying him, and of obtaining his own release. Such opportunities, it is said, he will easily meet with, unless the man be always on his guard, by fortifying himself with those means of defence which other charms afford, and by living agreeably to certain rules laid down for those who retain demons in their service. Hence these charms are never tried in these days, although many men in bye-gone times are said to have used them successfully. If you challenge a Singhalese to prove any of the absurd things he so confidently relates, and which, if true, must from their very nature be susceptible of proof, he will always appeal to the experience of the past ages, and declare that, 30 or 40 years ago, there were many men well skilled in these difficult and important classes of charms.

In the second class of charms, namely those intended to cure diseases, or to secure one from falling sick from the influence of demons and charms, there is a great variety, of which the principal are Bandena and Dehena. Bandena is a term, which simply means "binding" or a "bond," and although many of the Hooniyan and other charms are also sometimes called by the same name, yet it properly belongs only to those, by which diseases brought on by demons are cured. The number of these charms is very great, and we give below the names of a few:—

1. Maha Seyiyadu Bandena
2. Demalla Seyiyadu Bandena
3. Raja Gingili Bandena
4. Demalla Gingili Bandena
5. Cadiramala Bandena
6. Lanka Bandena
7. Wahalla Bandena
8. Canda Cumara Bandena
9. Maha Dewa Bandena
10. Hanuma Bandena
11. Scema Bandena
12. Rooban Cala Bandena
13. Cal-lu Bandena
14. Agni Rama Serra Bandena
15. Mahammadu Bandena
16. Seyiyadu Bandena
17. Subu Cama Bandena
18. Garukee Bandena
19. Brahma Bandena
20. Wilocha Bandena
21. Mulu Sanni Bandena
22. Dewa Sanni Bandena
23. Rawura Rama Bandena

DEHENAS are less powerful than Bandenas, but are still more numerous than either the Bandenas or any other class of Charms. They are made use of in curing slight diseases, and in removing in time any Tanicama influence from a man. Each Dehena consists of seven classes or divisions. The following are the names of a few of these charms.

1. Diagat Dehena
2. Ginigat Dehena
3. Sunakat Dehena
4. Canda Cumara Dehena
5. Attrottra Dehena
6. Randaney Dehena
7. Visnu Dehena
8. Hena Wali Dehena

When you try to convince a Demon-worshipper of the absurdity of his belief in charms and other Demon Ceremonies, the greatest difficulty you meet with is not so much any captious or cavilling arguments in defence of his faith and practice, as two other insuperable obstacles, which render all your arguments perfectly useless. One is a sort of mental apathy, an unenquiring, contented, and lethargic state of mind, satisfied with what is, and incurious or indifferent to learn any thing new—a state of mind, in which the man sometimes mechanically acquiesces in all that you say, and admits the force and truth of your arguments, without however his reason being at all convinced or his feelings affected. The other obstacle is, if possible, still more insurmountable, in as much as when you think you have nearly convinced him, and that you are in a fair way of converting him to the side of reason and truth, you are at once stopped by an argument, which he throws in your face, and which certainly you cannot answer,—an appeal to his own experience of what he has "seen with his own eyes," and what he is certain cannot be otherwise than as he thinks it is. He will tell you at the conclusion of your lecture, "Sir, all this may be true, indeed *very* true, *but* for what I have seen with these eyes of mine." If you ask him what those things may be which he has seen with "his own eyes," he will mention to you several instances of men, women, and children cured of sundry dangerous diseases by means of Charms and Demon Ceremonies, or of others who were suddenly struck down with disease by demon influence, and whom no medicine could cure until the Cattadiya performed a certain ceremony. If you try to argue with him on the possibility of any of these things happening in the ordinary course of nature without the agency of any demon or charm, he will give you his reasons against such a belief. He will say "Oh I have seen it with these two eyes of mine, and I know very well that it is so. It can't be otherwise. If my eyes and ears do not deceive me in other things of my daily life, why should they do so in this. Chance cannot do these things, nor the ordinary course of nature. If demons and demon-sickness, and demon-ceremonies be mere fictions, I should be more glad of it than you, because it would save my poor earnings for other purposes; but that they are not fictions, I have often found to my cost. Only the other day Sanchy Hamy, Tamby Appoo's wife, fell sick; and who cured her? To be sure, the Cattadiya. And why didn't Juanis Wederalla (physician) cure her, although he exhausted all his skill and art during four or five weeks? Abanchy Appoo practised Hooniyan spells on my uncle last year; and my uncle fell sick about 5 months afterwards. Could the Wederalla cure him? Did he cure him? Or, did any other demon ceremony cure him until the proper one, namely *Hooniyan Kepeema*, was performed. Didn't my uncle get better immediately after this ceremony? Didn't Abancby Appoo himself tell us afterwards that he had practised Hooniyan spells on my uncle?" The more you reason with him, the more unanswerable does he become, in as much as he believes in "his own eyes," "his own ears," and "his own judgment," much more than he can do in yours. Really, credulity and its parent, ignorance, are demons too powerful to be overcome by the mere charm of reason unassisted by the Jeewama of education.

Another difficulty, is a sort of simulating hypocrisy, which a demon worshipper assumes before you, if you are an Englishman. He agrees with all that you say, and condemns the system of demon-worship as a ridiculous absurdity, and while you are congratulating yourself in the idea that you have succeeded in convincing a couple of honest, sensible men of the propriety of abjuring demon-worship, they go away laughing at your own ignorance and simplicity, and at the same time charitably pitying you for being a Christian, for they are sure that, the moment you leave this world, you will go to the worst of all hells, the *Lokanantarika Narakaya.*

CHAPTER VI.

Demon Possession.

Where the belief in demoniac agency, even in matters of a trivial character, is so intense and universal, such a thing as demon possession, which was believed in even in more civilized countries till very lately, cannot be expected to be unknown. Hence, we believe, no Englishman will be surprised, when we say that there is scarcely a single village in the Island, in which there are not to be found at least half a dozen women, who are subject, at different intervals and during a considerable portion of their lives, to this influence, which, if it once comes upon a woman, will, it is said, last through the whole of her life, displaying itself now and then in active operation according to circumstances, unless removed by suitable means. These circumstances are generally the presence of the woman at the performance of any demon ceremony, or in the immediate neighbourhood of one, though performed at another's house; or if she happens to roast eggs, or meat, or to eat them roasted; or if she passes by a grave, not more than a day old, on a Saturday or Wednesday; or if she is present at the ceremony of reciting certain sermons of Buddha against demons called *Pirit,* especially of the last portion of these called *Aatanati Soottra.* In the case of some women, the demon influence is always ready to shew itself even on less important occasions, as for instance when they make *porri;* or when they go abroad on a Saturday or a Wednesday, especially during a Yama; or when they smell the smoke of *Dummala* resin; or when they hear the sound of a *Yak berray* (a drum used in demon ceremonies); and on other occasions equally trifling. Men are very seldom subject to this influence, and even of women it is generally the younger portion, who seem to have an attraction for the demons. This influence sometimes shews itself suddenly without there being any perceptible immediate cause for it.

The symptoms of demon possession vary at different times even in the same woman. In some cases she begins by complaining of weakness and faintness, accompanied sometimes by a sort of involuntary trèmor in her limbs and shoulders. She then sinks into a state of insensibility, as in a swoon, but continues ever and anon to gnash and grind her teeth, and now and then opens her eyes, and looks at the bystanders with a fierce angry stare, rolling the eyeballs so as to conceal the iris as much as possible, and to display only the whites of the eyes. Some women do not fall into swoons at all, but, get into a most excited state of frenzy, and shout and howl in the most remarkable manner, the *Hoo* sound being the most prominent, sometimes mentioning also the names of a demon or two, and screaming out that the demon would not be satisfied, unless an offering were made to him. Some attempt to run about. Some rush into the Dancing Ring, if a demon ceremony is taking place at the time, and wresting from the Cattadiya's hands the burning torch, dance away in the most violent manner. On these occasions the Cattadiya performs his incantations over the woman. and she recovers. If she is asked afterwards, whether she had any consciousness of what she said and did during her "madness," she of course says that she had not. During the frenzy she sometimes, but not often, uses very indecent language, although at all other times in her life she has never been heard to use, even by way of a joke among friends of her own sex, any expression unwarranted by good manners and the rules of decency and morality.

There is one woman that we know, who is subject to "demon possession" in a peculiar manner. She is a *Pattini Hamy* (priestess of the goddess Pattini Dewiyo), and wife of a Capua (priest of the gods.) Whenever this Capua happens to be engaged in any ceremony peculiar to the worship of the gods, his wife the Pattini Hamy, who is at home and at a distance from the scene of the ceremony, gets herself into this peculiar condition about 3 or 4 o'clock in the morning, at which time the Capua is engaged in a particularly important part of his ceremony. She does not shout nor attempt to run away like many of those already mentioned, but falls into a sort of partial swoon, during which, at short intervals of tii w, she moves her head from side to side very rapidly, muttering at the same time, or seeming to mutter, something quite inaudible. In this state she continues for about a quarter of an hour, and then falls into a sleep, which continues for nearly another quarter of an hour.

In the removal of this influence from a woman, mere incantations are supposed to be effectual no further, than in obtaining a momentary cure only; but when such incantations do not succeed even so far as this, a certain ceremony called *Pralaye Kireema* is performed. This consists in repeating certain charms over the woman, or more generally over a small quantity of water which is afterwards sprinkled over her; the immediate effect of this is to increase her frenzy to such a degree, that she pants and foams at the mouth, throwing her arms here and there in a most excited manner. The Cattadiya then speaks to her thus—"If it be true that demons must obey king Wissamonny, if it be true that Wissamonny's power is great; if it be true that the authority of Wissamonny, of the gods, and of Buddha still prevails in the world, then I command thee, demon, in the name of Buddha, his priests, and his doctrines, to declare, who thou art, and why thou afflictest this human creature in this manner." Upon this, the woman becomes, if possible, still more frantic and "mad," and mentions the name of some demon, such as Calu Yakseya or Reeri Yakseya, and adds, "I want an offering of a human sacrifice; I will not leave her without having one." The offering is then promised by the recitation of a charm, and the Cattadiya having taken a little water in the palm of his hand, and having pronounced a charm over it, throws it over her face, on which she recovers in 5 or 6 minutes more. The promised offering—a cock being substituted for the human sacrific—is also given by the performance of a certain appropriate demon ceremony in 3 or 4 weeks' time or sometimes sooner. If, after this the woman again shews symptoms of demon possession, the demon is "bound and nailed" to a tree. This business is performed thus—a nail made of *Pas lo*, having been submitted to the necessary Jeewama, is driven into the trunk of a large living tree. A Kan-ya Nool thread, also charmed and subjected to the same Jeewama, coloured yellow with saffron, and knotted during the Jeewama, is coiled round the nail, the Cattadiya the whole time muttering charms. The demon is supposed by this means to be "bound and nailed." Sometimes, instead of nailing the demon to a tree, he is "imprisoned" in a small box made of lead, which is then thrown into the sea or a river. If neither of these avail, the last resource is to go to the temple called *Gala Cappu Dewale* at Alut Nuvera. What takes place there we have already described in a previous chapter. There the exorcism is supposed to be complete. But some women even after this last exorcism, get a relapse which then is considered to be incurable.

Demon possession is however not confined to Buddhists; women of the Roman Catholic faith are equally subject to it. When a Roman Catholic is suffering under demon possession, the exorcism is performed by the *Annevy*, a native officer of the Roman Catholic Church, or, if he fails by the Roman Catholic priest himself. On these occasions the cross and the images of the Saints being shewn to the woman, she is asked what they are. At this question some women begin to tremble, and try to avoid looking at them. By and bye by threats and prayers she is brought both to look at them, and to acknowledge what they are. The Lord's Prayer and the Prayer to the Virgin Mary are then read over her, each seven times ; after this, the charm called *Rattu Mandiram*, or binding charm, is written on a piece of paper, which, having been folded up into a small bundle and sprinkled with Holy Water, is suspended from the neck of the woman ; and the same charm is again pronounced over her. Some frankincense is then burnt and its smoke held under her face. The Annevy then addresses her in nearly these terms—"Leave this woman and go thy way. I charge thee, demon, in the name of the Father, the Son, and the Holy Ghost, in the name of the Virgin Mary, and of all the Saints. Leave her this instant, or thou shalt be punished severely." Sometimes the woman says, "No, I won't leave her." On one occasion about two years ago, a woman, being asked during the exorcism why the demon would not quit her, replied, "because she is the most beautiful woman in the village." At this stage of the business the woman is struck across her back with the tail of a Skate fish, over which the aforesaid Kattu mandiram charm had previously been pronounced; and if the demon still resist, the beating is repeated. After seven or eight blows the demon is overpowered, and the woman regains her senses.

It is said that with whatever strength of arm the fish tail or the cane be used, it will leave no marks of blows on the woman's back, and that, even if there happen to be any, these will entirely disappear in a few minutes, if the case be one of real demon possession. As we ourselves however have never had the good fortune to examine the back of a lady after such an operation, we cannot give the reader the benefit of our own evidence on the matter; we do indeed know one case, in which a very sensible husband, on seeing his wife beginning to shew symptoms of demon possession, immediately seized *Ilapota* or the housebrush,* and with it gave her right and left 20 or 30 smart blows, loudly exclaiming while doing so, "Is there a greater demon here than myself? I will teach thee, demon, who I am." In this case we saw on her back the marks of the blows as distinct and clear as possible. When we mentioned this to some of the bystanders as contradicting the opinion, which they all held on the subject, they told us, "Oh, but these will disappear in a few minutes. We know it very well. We have always fouud it so. Indeed it cannot be otherwise, unless the lady be shamming possession." Some of the more ingenious but equally orthodox of the party remarked that the person, who inflicted the

---

* A large number of the strong, wiry midribs or central nerves of the leaflets of a frond of cocoanut leaves, or of Areca leaves, being separated from the other parts of the leaflets, are tied up together into a bundle with a coir yarn at their thicker ends, and this is called *Ilapota.* It is used in the native houses for sweeping the floor, which is always done by the women. Men may use other sorts of brooms or brushes for the same purpose, but will never use this, as it is considered too low and mean a thing for a man to handle. The greatest disgrace that one man can bring on another is to strike him with an Ilapota, though it be but a gentle and single blow.

blows in this case, being but an ordinary man and not a Capua, and no charms or invocations being made to any demons or gods for assistance, the marks of the blows might or might not remain, without in either case compromising the correctness of the doctrine.

The following is the charm *Kattu Mandiram* used by the Annevy in the exorcism of demons.

"Oh God! May my head, neck, and throat be under the protection of the Father, the Son, and the Holy Ghost! May they be under the protection of the powerful Commander, the Archangel St. Michael and his sword! May my right shoulder be under the protection of the Archangel Gabriel and his sword! May my left shoulder be under the protection of the Archangel Raphael and his sword! May my breast and back be under the protection of all the Saints! May my navel be under the protection of the twelve Apostles! May my private parts be under the protection of the 11,000 virgins! May my feet, legs, the soles of my feet, and the 20 fingers and toes with their nails be under the protection of all the Saints! I have taken God to be my protection. I have brought the Ten Commandments to my mind. In the name of the Father, the Son, and the Holy Ghost, who sit on a throne of glory resplendent with the effulgence of starry gems, in the Holy Name of the Divine Mother, who obeys the Divine Will, I expel all inimical demons, who come from the East, the West, the North, and the South; demons who come from hell beneath the earth, from the five points of the sky, and the sixteen points of the world. I bind all poisonous creatures, be they beasts, birds, or fishes; be they those, that creep upon their bellies, or that move on their legs, or that fly through the air by their wings. I bind elephants, horses, bears, lions, tigers, and all other animals, that may be dangerous. I bind all these, so that Angam, Pilli, Hooniyan, the dangers of *passing over*, and all the demons, preteyas, and the diseases caused by these, may break, break, flee, flee,* and be expelled again and

* Repetition of the same word, especially words like those in the text, is a very common practice in charms, because such repetition is supposed to increase the force and efficacy of a charm.

again. I bind by the divine power of the Cross. I bind by the power of the five divine wounds. I bind by the authority of the Angels. I bind so as to render the bond indissoluble. By the divine power of the Cross. Amen, Jesu."

This remarkable phenomenon in the conduct of thousands of Singhalese women throughout the Island can not, we believe, be wholly explained away by the supposition, that *all* these women are only humbugging every body by shamming madness, merely for the unreasonable pleasure of putting themselves in a state of frantic excitement or of assumed insensibility; an explanation the more unsatisfactory, when it is considered that this peculiarity is often found even in respectable old ladies verging upon 60 and 70—mothers of large families—very respectable, sober, honest, modest characters—who, so far from wishing to simulate madness or demon possession, have always appeared to be quite incapable of such wilful folly. Further, we have often had ample opportunities of minutely observing every thing said and done by one or two such persons when under "possession," and although on such occasions we were very anxious to convince all around us that all this was nothing but shamming, or at best the effects of an excited and morbid imagination, we yet never failed to perceive much, that could not be reconciled with any idea of imposture, and however much we endeavoured to believe in their being counterfeit, we never succeeded in fully convincing our reason.

We must however state here in justice to these old ladies, that their symptoms of possession were not exactly like those we have generally described above; they did not call upon demons, nor shout and cry, but simply sank down on the ground as in a fit of insensibility, and then continued, now and then, to tremble very violently, gnashing their teeth and rolling their eyeballs. In this state they generally remain about three quarters of an hour, and then sit up as if awaking from a sleep. For nearly a day after this they complain of weakness, and after that are as well as ever and about their household duties as usual. In other respects they do not seem to be suffering from any disease, but on the contrary are in the enjoyment of good health.

Many of the so-called demon possessions are without doubt mere shams, grown perhaps fashionable among a certain class of ignorant coquettish young women; but some, forming of course a small minority, do not, we are inclined to believe, admit of this explanation, if we can place any reliance on our own senses and judgment. Whether or not real demon possessions, such as those mentioned in the New Testament, do take place in these days too, we do not know; but if, as we think, they do not, this remarkable phenomenon can be explained only by attributing it to involuntary Mesmerism and what has been called the Cataleptic trance. But the wonder is that it should be so frequent and common in this Island, in so much as to exceed in the number of occasions and the number of persons affected, all the demoniac possessions or what were so called, which have ever been recorded as having occurred in all other parts of the world put together, from the beginning of the Christian era down to this day. We do not know what are the causes which induce the mesmeric state in a person; but if an excited imagination, overwrought feelings of superstitious fear, and an intense fervid belief in the existence and the attributes of demons, combined with very weak, credulous, timid minds, can do it, then all these may be found in a high degree in a large majority of Singhalese females.

However, whatever may be the cause, whether it be mesmeric agency, or mere shamming, still the fact is remarkable in either case. For, if Mesmerism or the Cataleptic trance, be the cause, why or how it should be found in such active operation in so many instances in this Island during every year, would be an interesting subject of inquiry, nor on the other hand can the other imputed cause (if cause it be in all those instances), viz., a morbid propensity, which leads women to counterfeit demon possession, appear to be a matter less remarkable, in as much as it shews the low state of education which exists among the Singhalese.

CHAPTER VII.

Dreadful Consequences of a belief in Demon Influence.

The reader, who has had the patience to follow us thus far, will, we believe, have his mind impressed with one principal idea, viz., that credulity and superstitious fear exercise so powerful an influence over an uneducated Singhalese, as to blind his reason entirely, the moment his mind reverts to demons or to any thing relating to them. Without such an hypothesis, it is difficult to believe that there are men now living, who honestly and sincerely say and believe that they have actually seen demons, and have thereby fallen sick, from which they recovered only by the aid of charms and demon-ceremonies, and that by similar means it is in the power of any man at any time to inflict disease or death or some other misfortune on another. The account we have given of these spells, and of the wonderful virtues believed by the Singhalese to be inherent in them will, we believe, only raise a smile of contempt and pity in an Englishman's face; but if the Englishman knew to what deplorable results this belief often leads, his look of contempt would be changed to one of horror.

In many of the inland villages of this Island factions, quarrels, bloodshed, and crime have often been the consequences of this belief in charms, especially in Hooniyan charms. One family living at bitter enmity with another, with all their respective relatives and friends ranged on either side and each trying to injure the other in every possible way, by perjury, litigation, theft, and assault, turning peaceful villages into scenes of misery, and harmless peasants into ruthless murderers, and thereby perpetuating the feud from one generation to another, are not things of rare occurrence; and all this, either because a young man of one family happened on one occasion to prepare Hooniyan charms against a young woman of another family, because he could not get her to marry him; or because a man fell sick soon after an unfriendly neighbour had been seen to bury a charmed image under his garden gate, or for some other similar reason. Among many instances of this kind which have come under our own notice, we will give here one or two for the benefit of the reader, from which it will appear that, if the power and influence of demons are to be perceived anywhere in these Hooniyan matters, it must be in the miseries brought on many an honest and happy family by their credulity.

In the district of Caltura in the Western Province of the Island, there lived some years ago a man, we will call Hendrick Appoo, with his family consisting of his wife, three sons, and one daughter. The sons were grown up men, married and having children. The daughter was the youngest and still unmarried. Hendrick Appoo was considered by his fellow villagers to be a rich man, that is, he had some 15 or 20 head of cattle, and about 6 or 7 acres of land scattered here and there in the village in small pieces of a rood or two each; and he had too his own paddyfield and sweet potatoe and betel plantations with 50 or 60 cocoanut trees and 7 or 8 jack trees: it was also supposed that he had in cash about 2 or 3 hundred Rixdollars (£15 or £22 10*s.*) His father had been a Widhane Aratchy, and so he was a village aristocrat. In short, he was a "Country gentleman." He had a neighbour we shall call Harmanis Appoo, also well thought of by his neighbours as a man well to do in the world. This man had only two children, both unmarried, young men of good character. As he and Hendrick Appoo were men in the same rank of life, and especially as they both happened to be nearly equal to each other in the respectability of their pedigrees (an essential point in the matrimonial arrangements of the Singhalese,) it was proposed and agreed between them that the eldest son of the one should marry the daughter of the other. The proposal met with the approbation of nearly all the members of both the families; and so both the families became very friendly and attached to each other, assisting each other in various small matters, and in short living on the most intimate and happy terms with each other, as is usual on the proposal, and before the consummation, of a marriage between any two families. Of course the two young persons, who were most interested in the matter, were not consulted, for they had no consent to give or withhold; such things being always managed for them by their parents. But sometime afterwards Aberan Appoo, a maternal uncle of the girl, and a man who was most scrupulously punctilious in matters of family pedigrees, returned from Saffragam where he had been trading for 4 or 5 months, and now for the first time hearing of the intended marriage determined to frustrate it, because he found a flaw in the pedigree of Harmanis Appoo, viz., that the father of his grandmother had been married to the descendant of a bastard slave. This in Aberan Appoo's opinion was an insuperable obstacle to the marriage, and so he set himself to work upon the family pride of his brother-in-law and his sister, in which he succeeded so well, that the match was soon broken off, and all intercourse between the two families ceased. Harmanis Appoo taking this as a mortal and unpardonable affront resolved to have his revenge. So he went to a Cattadiya in the Southern Province, and got him to prepare a Hooniyan charm against the young woman, and returning home, quietly waited for the result, of which he had not the slightest doubt. Curiously enough, just two months after this, the young woman died from the effects of a fever, which she had contracted through exposure to bad weather. Old Harmanis chuckling at this and too vain to hold his tongue confided to one or two of his confidential friends, how he had taken his revenge on Hendrick. Hendrick himself had heard before this of the other's visit to the Southern Province, but had never learned the purpose of the journey. As usual with prudent parents especially when a marriage proposal breaks off, he had taken every possible precaution, by means of charms and other amulets, to secure his daughter from the dangers arising from Hooniyan and other demon-influences; but when he heard, the day after the funeral of his child, of what Harmanis had been boasting privately to his friends, it confirmed him in his previous suspicions, and roused all the evil nature in him. These suspicions were still further confirmed by the discovery of a small wooden image buried under one of the front steps of his Verandah. So, a few days afterwards, he and his three sons with two others, hired with drams of arrack for the occasion, quietly repaired in the dark to Harmanis' house, and severely assaulted him, his wife, his sons, and all others who were in his house. The next day they went before a Magistrate and swore an affidavit, that he (Hendrick Appoo) and his sons, while returning home one night from Morottoo with a large sum of money, had been waylaid by Harmanis Appoo and his sons with 5 or 6 other men, who assaulted them and robbed them of their money. Harmanis also swore an affidavit, stating in it the actual truth, with the addition of a robbery and burglary committed on his property. Each was supported by false evidence, and both the complaints having been investigated by the Magistrate, both were dismissed by him, as neither appeared to him to be true. A few weeks after this, Harmanis with a party of his friends repaired to his enemy's house, and assaulted him and all his people with clubs, knives and rice-pounders (long wooden pestles), and many on both sides were severely wounded. The matter was tried before the Supreme Court, but the jury acquitted the accused. Then for a period of nearly four years the two families were engaged in a series of civil lawsuits arising out of certain bonds, in all of which judgment was given against Hendrick—bonds, which came into existence only after the rupture between the two families, Hendrick having never borrowed a farthing from the other on a bond or without a bond. And yet the deeds purported to have been duly executed before a notary! Before execution was granted in the last of these cases, the two sons of Harmanis were found one evening lying dead in a neighbouring rice field, with marks of violence on them: and although every possible exertion was made by those in authority to discover the murderers, no trace of truthful evidence could be had, and although a dozen relatives of the deceased swore to its being the work of Hendrick's sons, there did not appear any trustworthy evidence whatever against any one. The case was however tried upon the evidence of these relatives, but the jury at once acquitted the prisoners, Hendrick himself and his sons. In a few weeks afterwards every thing belonging to Hendrick was sold by the Fiscal to satisfy the execution in the civil suits mentioned above, and as there still remained a large balance due, Hendrick was incarcerated in a debtor's prison. Harmanis lost both his sons, and got a considerable sum of money recovered upon his bonds, but did not live long enough to enjoy it, as in about a year's time he was poisoned, and died a miserable death. The suspected culprits were not brought to punishment, as there was not a tittle of legal evidence against them. Thus these two families, who had lived comfortably and respectably in their quiet village for a long time, were ruined; and other villagers, who had taken part in their quarrels, did not fare better. Certainly a Hooniyan Charm, viewed in this light, must appear to be a thing of greater malignity, than the Cattadiya and his books represent it to be in its direct consequences.

The following case is not less characteristic. It happened in a village not very far from Colombo. Andris had a lawsuit with Siman Nydey respecting a small piece of land, not worth more than £2 or £3, and judgment was pronounced in favour of Siman. Andris, resolving upon revenge, had recourse to witchcraft, and a Hooniyan being prepared, the image was buried at night in the yard of Siman Nydey's house, opposite to the front door. Unfortunately for Andris, he was detected in the very act, and was seized by the inmates of the house, who headed by Siman, joined in giving him a good thrashing. Not content however with this they cut off a bunch of plantains from a tree close by, and placed it beside Andris, who lay on the ground, bound hand and foot and smarting from the blows he had received. The Police Widhane was then sent for, and on his arrival Siman charged Andris with intruding into his dwelling garden at night and stealing plantains from it. All Singhalese know well that Englishmen never punish people for practising Hooniyan or any other sort of witchcraft, and hence this fictitious charge of theft. The Magistrate tried the case, and the man being found guilty was sentenced to a month's imprisonment with hard labour. Before he could return home from the jail, his enemy Siman, wishing to pay him in kind, consulted a Cattadiya, and got a Hooniyan ceremony performed against him. On his return from the jail, the first thing Andris heard was a rumour of Siman's having been seen going one night towards a graveyard in company with another man, who carried with him a cock concealed under his Saron cloth, together with some live coals in a broken chatty. Of course Andris immediately understood what it meant, and perhaps thinking within himself that "the best of all charms is a club-charm" (a popular Singhalese saying), the next evening about the time that Siman, who was a toddy drawer, generally returned home after drawing Toddy in the neighbouring hamlet, he shouldered his Mamottie (*Anglice* hoe) and walked along the path, by which he knew the other would come. When he saw Siman approach, he concealed himself behind a bush, and, as he passed, with a single blow of the Mamottie, struck him to the ground. The unfortunate man's skull was completely fractured, and he lived only 3 days. Andris was tried before the Supreme Court, and being found guilty, expiated his crime on the gallows. Even after this the two families had many quarrels and lawsuits, but none productive of consequences so serious.

A young man, who was a "rising" astrologer, fell sick, and his physicians did all they could for him, but without any effect. Day by day he grew worse, and was fast approaching his last end. From the first, the illness was attributed to demon influence, and nothing, that charms and Cattadiyas and Balicarayas and Buddhist Priests and Capuas could do, was left untried. The patient however grew no better, and at last he died. The suddenness of the disease, and the speedy death it resulted in, were matters of suspicion even in the minds of the neighbours, and much more certainly in that of the father of the deceased. The old man suspected another astrologer, who lived in the same village, of having practised Hooniyan Charms against his son, and all doubt was removed from his mind, when he heard a few days afterwards that a certain Cattadiya, who lived in a distant village, was seen, some three or four months before, going to the house of the astrologer late in the evening, and in such a manner as if he wished to go unseen. Whether this was true or a mere invention of some unprincipled villager, the old man did not care to enquire, he was but too ready to believe what he had all along strongly suspected. When he heard it, he was maddened with anger. He could not bear the idea of his beloved son being snatched away from him by foul play. He had taken great pains and had been put to considerable expence in training his favorite son to the profession of an astrologer, and to be thus suddenly disappointed, just as he was about to reap the reward of all his labours in the fame and glory of his son, was past all human endurance, especially the endurance of our old carpenter, who seldom raised his chisel or his adze without consulting an astrologer for an auspicious hour. The old man burning with rage and resentment, resolved to have his revenge. He had a neighbour who, being something of a sportsman, had a gun. He had also a mango tree in his compound, the fruit of which was every day devoured by monkeys, so he asked his neighbour for the loan of his gun to drive off these troublesome robbers. Every day, when monkeys were seen on or near his mango tree, he took out the gun, loaded it carefully, and first levelling it at the intruding monkeys, turned and fired it in a different direction ; for it was a great sin to kill animals, especially monkeys. Besides, he was an *Upasakaya.**

* An *Upasakaya* is a religious Buddhist, or at least one who professes to be so, by the observance of certain precepts of Buddha called *Sil* or *Seela*. These precepts or obligations are.

1. Do not take away life.
2. Do not take that which is not given.
3. Do not commit adultery.
4. Do not speak that which is not true.
5. Do not use intoxicating liquors.
6. Do not use solid food after mid-day.
7. Do not attend at dancing, singing, music, and masquerades.
8. Do not adorn the body with flowers, perfumes, or unguents.
9. Do not use seats above the prescribed height.
10. Do not receive gold or silver.

Of these the first five, called *Pan Sil* or *Pancha Seela*, are considered to be obligatory on all. These five with the next three, forming eight Obligations, are called *Ata Sil*. One professing to observe these eight is called an *Upasak*

So this sort of shooting at monkeys continued for three or four weeks. One evening, as the astrologer was returning home from another village, and was moving along a footpath flanked on both sides by thick bushes, he was shot by somebody concealed among the bushes and lived only a few hours. The Jury, who tried the old carpenter, at once acquitted him, as, although there was as usual a good deal of false evidence put in, which from its nature was not, and could not be, believed, there was not a tittle of trustworthy evidence against him, excepting the mere fact of his having had at his house a gun borrowed from a neighbour to shoot monkeys. But all the villagers knew to a certainty that the old man was the murderer.

Instances like the above can be multiplied by hundreds, if necessary ; but the few already cited will, we think, be sufficient to give the reader some idea of the nature of the evils, which a belief in the power of charms often produces among our countrymen ; a belief, which is not confined to those, whom we are in the habit of styling common people, but which prevails equally, though with less serious consequences, among Singhalese of a higher class and condition, with the exception of a very few well educated intelligent people, not exceeding, we firmly believe, four or five hundred individuals in the whole island.

There is a peculiarity, very general among the Singhalese, that if an European questions a Cattadiya about any particular department of his art, he will give just such answers, as he thinks will be most in accordance with the opinions of the querist, as far as it can be done without wholly condemning the entire system ; but whenever there appears to be no chance of avoiding this last dilemma, he will make every possible excuse to make a hasty retreat, without entangling himself in the difficulties of a discussion, in which he knows he will not be able to triumph. If an Englishman tells an advocate of Demonism that charms and Demon Ceremonies are mere follies ; that no benefit whatever can be derived from them ; that they are mere impostures intended to delude the ignorant ; and that the most learned Cattadiya cannot satisfactorily prove that they possess any of the powers ascribed to them ; the answer most probably will be—"Sir, I don't know much about these things myself; my forefathers have believed in them, my neighbours still do so, and what is good for them cannot, I think, do any harm to myself. Possibly much of what you say may be true, and certainly a great deal of what now goes under the name of charms is spurious, and many of the Cattadiyas are ignorant impostures. Really, Sir, I don't understand these things well, but there may be some, who can perhaps satisfy you on the subject, though I cannot." Or he will say—"Sir, I don't know whether these things be true or false. When we fall sick, we try every means within our reach of getting better. We worship Buddha, the gods, and the demons, all at once, to take our chance of recovering from the sickness through the help of some of them. All my countrymen do so, and I am only doing like them." The demeanour of the man during this conversation is like that of one, who has been convinced of the absurdity of his worship, and who is anxious to profit by the advice of a superior, although he evinces considerable impatience at being stopped, and is anxious to get away as soon as possible. The moment he turns his back however, he will go away laughing at his own skill in answering so well and cursing, or at least pitying the Englishman for being an infidel and a Christian. Hence many an Englishman is led to believe that Demon Worship has not at present a firm hold of the minds of a portion of the people, and that it is upheld amongst a few merely because custom, or habit has made it familiar to them. Nothing can be more erroneous than this opinion; for so far from a portion of the people being indifferent to Demon Worship from a conviction that it is an absurdity, we believe there is not (excepting 4 or 5 hundred well educated men in the whole Island) one Singhalese man, who believes in any thing more firmly than in Demonism. In Colombo and its immediate neighbourhood alone, where the superstition does not command many *zealous* votaries, there are some few who have no great faith in charms, or who, though believing in them, have no opportunity of reducing that belief into practice in the form of Demon ceremonies ; but in all other parts of the Island, Demonism exercises a more commanding influence over the every day life and thoughts of a Singhalese, than any other *ism* that we know of.
